future libraries
future catalogues

PAT ODDY
Head of Cataloguing, The British Library

Library Association Publishing
London

© Pat Oddy 1996

Published by
Library Association Publishing
7 Ridgmount Street
London WC1E 7AE

First published 1996

British Library Cataloguing in Publication Data

A catalogue record for this book is available from the British Library

ISBN 1-85604-161-1

Typeset from author's disk in 10/13pt Baskerville and Poppl-Laudatio by Library Association Publishing
Printed and made in Great Britain by Bookcraft (Bath) Ltd, Midsomer Norton, Avon

CONTENTS

ACKNOWLEDGMENTS

Many people and institutions have contributed to this book, some of whom I would like to take the opportunity of thanking here.

The British Library has my gratitude not only for accepting the pressures which the writing of the book placed on my ability to carry out my day job, but also for giving me the opportunity to work on so many interesting and invigorating developments in cataloguing and catalogues over the last years. The experiences I have had have assisted immeasurably in the analysis of the problems facing cataloguing; I hope that the British Library will be able to benefit from the strategy for dealing with those problems which this book presents. I must of course make clear that the views and opinions expressed are entirely my own and are not necessarily shared by the British Library.

The staff of the Cataloguing Department at the British Library have been an invaluable source of support and ideas. I would particularly like to thank Paul Bunn, Alan Danskin, Lucy Evans and Sally Strutt for their help during the past year.

The catalyst for the book was Thomas Mann, whose writings on research methods brought vividly back to my mind the vital interplay between catalogues and collections.

Finally and most importantly, I owe Michael Gorman a professional and personal debt, the size of which he knows.

Pat Oddy

PROLOGUE

Communications are the technological growth area of the 1990s. Every day, it seems, we read and hear that in the future we will carry out our everyday business of shopping, reading newspapers, ordering pizzas, even voting, from a computer in the comfort of our home. No matter that we can do all these things already by other means, and usually much more easily, efficiently and economically than through a computer and a phone line. Why persist in clinging to your Citroën 2CV, when you could be soaring down the information superhighway in a Porsche?

Libraries are in the business of communication, the business of exchange of information, and technological developments have always been seized upon by librarians, whenever they offer the opportunity to carry out that information exchange more speedily and efficiently. Catalogues have benefited from the introduction of more flexible methods of searching and displaying; reference work from the publication of indexes, abstracts and other works of reference on CD-ROM; acquisitions units through the increasing exchange of electronic information with publishers. Libraries welcome new media and new ways of communicating information, and library users know that they now house not just books, but videos, sound recordings, even access to online information services.

Despite the prevalence of the printed word as a significant and stable means of communicating, there is apparently great popular uncertainty as to its future. A recent poll carried out for the BBC's 'Bookworm' programme discovered that two out of three people believe that books will be obsolete by the year 2010.[1] Articles abound on the 'virtual library', that great digitized Utopia where all information and information about information will be held in electronic form. Librarians would be foolish not to consider seriously the implications of these ideas for a society in which printed matter forms the major component of most general library collections, in which libraries with walls play an important part in our communities, and in which sustained reading and the ability to reason and analyse are prized as social goods. Are these values in conflict with those of the all-electronic future? Louis Rossetto, the co-founder of *Wired* seems to think so:

> Written information is a relatively new phenomenon. Depositing it and being able to reference it centuries later is not common human experience. In some ways what is happening with online is a return to our earlier oral tradition. In other ways, it is utterly new, a direct connection of minds. Humans have always been isolated, and now we're starting to see electronic connections generating an intellectual organism of their own, literally a quantum leap beyond our experience with consciousness.[2]

A surface reading suggests that if this is the case then libraries do indeed have a big problem justifying their continued existence, and cataloguers even more so – for what are we about if not the referencing of common human experience so that it can later be found with ease? Digging down deeper, however, some seeds of doubt occur. Written information may be a relatively new phenomenon in the great scheme of things, but the organization of thought and ideas into logical and understandable patterns is not. The oral tradition is, indeed, a supreme example of such organization. Language is structured so as to make it comprehensible; stories and histories which are passed orally from generation to generation are of necessity unusually highly structured in order to be more easily committed to memory. Cave paintings, or artefacts such as the Bayeux tapestry, tell a story in a structured sequence of pictures. Oral and visual information was structured precisely so that it could be referenced later – Shakespeare's plays were originally recalled and written down from memory, as were the Scandinavian sagas. All means of communication involve a direct interplay of minds; words typed on a computer keyboard and sent electronically are essentially no more direct than words written on paper and sent through the mail or words spoken down a telephone line.

Nor does one means of communication disappear when a new form arrives on the scene: we still exchange information orally through song, drama and comedy, conveyed through the media of live performance, radio, or sound recording; visually through picture and film, conveyed through television or videos; through the written word in fiction, fact and poetry, conveyed on paper, fiche, or online. All media continue to exist for as long as there is a communication need which they fulfil more effectively than any other, at one particular time and place. Organized information is the great constant in human society; the media through which that organized information is communicated merely multiply and contract as society matures. Whilst they fulfil a need, there is no reason whatsoever why words printed on paper should disappear – unless we will it.

The library has been defined as 'A place set apart to contain books for reading, study or reference'.[3] Enlarged to encompass the variety of other media available now, in the past, and in the future, the definition is broad and strong and embraces the direct communication of human mind with human mind. Each library is defined by the needs of the community it serves and by which it is funded. Each library has a collection of materials, which may be in one or in many forms, but all acquired, listed and made available to assist the user of the collection in meeting his or her needs, whether for information, leisure or research.

Libraries are facing the challenge of the virtual library and the possible collapse of their traditional methods of the systematic organization of knowledge and information at a time when they have been seriously weakened by years of brutal change in the social, political and economic life of the UK. These changes have had a huge impact on the public services, forcing a fundamental shift in their value systems away from the satisfaction of the needs of the user in the community towards the satisfaction of the needs of the individual in the market place. Libraries are confused and disoriented, unsure of their future and of the viability of their established principles.

In 1620 Francis Bacon ranked printing as one of the three great inventions that had changed the world. It is hard to determine what the world would have been like without it, but we can hazard the guess that humans would have lived more isolated, insecure, threatened lives, lacking the ability to learn about, understand and accept the differences between them, and also the things that bind them together. The virtual library, were it ever to displace the real library, would take us back into that dark and isolated world, would help to break down the communication of human mind with human mind, would be a fitting testament to the increasingly insecure and threatened lives we live in a society driven by market forces.

It is my contention in this book that the concept of the virtual library is a chimera. Librarians are hungry to grasp at the mirage it offers of the power to undo, at a stroke, the evil of years of underfunding and cuts, by offering access to everything, for everyone, for free. It is not going to happen. If we allow ourselves to be seduced, the attraction will indeed be fatal to the professional values at the core of libraries and the organization of knowledge.

The changes that have taken place in society, and above all the dominance of the market ethos, cannot and will not be eradicated overnight. It is foolish to think that librarians can retreat behind the comfort of old values, pull the sheets over their heads and hope that better days will come. Nor can we sit back and take comfort in the thought that it's not our fault. If we care about libraries and the part they play in our communities we have to rethink our values, and rethink our strategies for realizing those values within the reality of the current social and economic climate. It is the purpose of this book to contribute to that analysis by looking at the heart of the library – its catalogue.

Without a collection, there is no catalogue. Without a catalogue, a collection cannot achieve its maximum good. To find a future for cataloguing, we first need to look at the future library collection – what it will consist of, where it will be housed, and how it will be used. We will then investigate the future catalogue, and how it can be most effectively structured to exploit the collection, and most efficiently created to exploit the resources available to us.

The intention of the chapters ahead is try to map out a practical way forward for cataloguing and catalogues in the 'Information Age'. First we must look at the social, political and economic environment within which the real library lives.

References

1 *Observer*, 26 November 1995, 3.
2 *Guardian*, 3 January 1995.
3 *The shorter Oxford English dictionary*, Oxford, Clarendon Press, 1978.

CHAPTER 1

SETTING THE SCENE

'Altruism and the civilising values of an inclusive society have been sacrificed on the altar of self-interest, of choice, of opting out and of individualism.'[1]

The fragmentation of society

From the time of the Industrial Revolution, but most particularly in
the post-war era of political consensus from 1945 to 1979, technological developments served to bind and reinforce the common
social experience of the citizens of these islands. Television channels and radio stations extended their coverage rapidly, but were
few in number and broadcast nationally rather than locally. Almost
all major newspapers had a national readership and circulation,
giving a countrywide currency to the events and stories they
reported. Basic utilities and services were owned by and accountable to the public, their employees covered by national conditions
of work and pay.

In the last 15 years, however, society has become increasingly
fragmented as the crude imposition of an unregulated competitive
market has chipped away at these shared cultural bonds. Cable and
satellite broadcasting, in harness with the video recorder, increasingly mean that the nation no longer watches the same television
programmes at the same time and discusses them together at
school, at work and in the pub the next day. It does not collectively
watch national events, when the rights to those events have been
sold to broadcasters whose programmes many people cannot, or
do not choose to, receive. Across the board, the public services are
dismembered and those that cannot be fattened for privatization

----

are starved of funding to the point where they aspire to do little more than provide a rump service to those who cannot choose to go elsewhere.

Broadcasting can serve as just one instance of the ground on which the battle between the public and the private sector, between individual and collective rights, has been fought. Here, as elsewhere, the argument centres on choice, and the belief that healthy competition will extend and enhance choice. But how likely is it that programme planners concerned with increasing their market share would have discovered, for example, any public demand for a series of programmes about strange plants? Without a public service broadcasting organization, David Attenborough's popular 'The private life of plants' would never have seen the light of day – and our society and culture is the richer for such programmes. One of the most interesting findings to come out of the 'People and programmes' report on the future programming strategy of the BBC is that three-quarters of the public believe its most important function is education, in the broadest sense of catering for 'the thirst for knowledge'. The public itself intuitively recognizes that publicly funded services are there to lead, not to follow; to ensure qualitative choice, not merely quantitative. As with broadcasting, so with that other provider of food for the mind, the library. It is that qualitative choice that is expensive to provide, and which is often not commercially viable to provide.

The only choice that comes cheap is no choice. The market will provide only what will keep the wheels of business turning, and for those who aspire to something other than what the market provides, the ability to exercise choice is only made possible through publicly funded, publicly accessible services. The argument that a democratic, capitalist society enhances choice can and should be used to defend and even extend public services, but sadly it is almost invariably used to push society further into the arms of a market which paradoxically restricts choice for the present and demand for choice in the future.

In recent years, each one of the public services has been forced to play a numbers game in which public money is granted, in decreasing amounts, for increased efficiency and productivity in its own quasi-market – a game with rules that are largely irrelevant to the kind of goals a public service wishes to achieve. Playing this macabre game, each service produces its own statement of its core values, twisted and misshapen to conform to the demands of the 'market', in strategic plans, corporate plans and business plans by the barrow load.

The threat to professional values

A whole range of public services – education, health, community care, social security – have turned into quasi-markets, and the role of government, at national or local level, has changed from provider to purchaser of these services. These structural changes have brought about a dislocation of the fundamental value systems of the public services, causing severe stress to the professional staff they employ. Everywhere attempts are being made to break the influence of professional groupings and put control in the hands of managers at the local, institutional level. In the Civil Service, pay and grading of staff will soon cease to be agreed at national level and will be delegated to individual departments and agencies. Schools are encouraged to break their link with local authorities and become grant-maintained. Hospitals aspire to Trust status.

The imposition of private sector values on a public service, professional constituency has had some disastrous consequences. As one example, 'gagging clauses' have prevented health workers and college lecturers talking to the press in any way which could be considered critical of their institutions. This is an entirely inappropriate and alien culture for those employed in the public service professions. Public servants have strong allegiances to their professions, which operate outside the control of the specific institutions in which they are employed. These allegiances harmonize well with concepts of public accountability and profession-wide pay and conditions, but ill with institutional strategies which seek to identify the individual with corporate aims, mission statements and competition in a quasi-market. Organizational structures and hierarchies within a school or a library do not necessarily mirror the actual power system present among professional staff, and the cultures within these institutions are very difficult to change except through the professional group. Professional and institutional goals are increasingly out of step and stresses build as staff are forced to choose between professional ideals and institutional realities.

The constant demand that increases in funding be offset by increased productivity and efficiency has led to the development of performance targets which are often entirely inappropriate to the service provided and incompatible with the values of those providing it. Police forces, for example, have adopted targets which are based on crime clear-up rates – despite the fact that the public is more concerned with crime prevention than cure; hospitals demonstrate that they have carried out more operations on more people in less time; schools and universities show that more students are achieving better examination results than ever before. At the same time, we are aware that crime is not decreasing, the health of the nation is not improving, and standards of education and literacy are not as high as we would like them to be. The increasingly apparent reality is that the self-regulating market cannot be an appropriate model for basic public services.

Never mind the quality, feel the bandwidth

Whilst libraries have been preoccupied with meeting the challenge of fundamental change to the social and political system in which they operate, the information explosion seems to have crept up on us from nowhere. A true child of its time, the 'Information Age' treats information as a thing, a quantifiable object that can be bought and sold in the market like any other commodity. Not only is information a commodity, but we have invested it with such a degree of importance that in some strange way 'information' is now seen as a necessity of life and the amount of 'information' available as a measure of the health and wealth of society. No matter that the amount of new information actually required in the ongoing business of daily life is, for most people, infinitesimal even on the broadest interpretation of the term, and that whatever we do need is usually very readily available by existing means of communication such as the telephone, fax, printed material and personal questioning – a computer and modem is the latest 'must have' consumer toy. The library is the place where individual needs for knowledge and information are met through the collective provision and interpretation of resources; technological developments which put the individual consumer directly in touch with a global information market-place create an apparently barren future for this particular public service.

In the drive to increase productivity and improve economic strength, the private sector has invested heavily in technological development. Within the public sector too technology has been used to increase productivity and efficiency, but with the primary objective of improving the value of the service provided to the public. Libraries, for example, automated rapidly; the possibility of record sharing and distribution increased exponentially, and users had catalogues which were current, potentially well-maintained, and amenable to a much wider range of search strategies. The collections could be used more effectively, and the library increased the value of the service it provided. The computerized catalogues, though, unlike their print and fiche predecessors, were only searchable at the library. Now the computer is moving out of the office, into the home and on to the road as the growth in electronic communication brings the library catalogue direct to a screen near you. The electronic evangelists believe that all this points to the sure and certain fact that the Internet is the library of the future.

The idea is current that the Internet is a 'good thing' because it is free, because it is accessible to anyone and everyone, and because it is essentially anarchic and libertarian. The spirit of the 60s lives on, despite all that Thatcherism and Reaganomics have thrown at us. Unfortunately, the reality is somewhat different. As Patrick R. Penland has said, 'An electronic world cannot be run by a 'hippie' mentality, even if it is in the tribal village of mass media communication.'[2] The disorderly, ungovernable infant that began life in the US military establishment and grew up amongst the academic fraternity has now become a global, multi-million pound business. It's still the same old story – technology responds and develops according to market-led priorities and to achieve economic rather than social ends.

The ideal underpinning the electronic information revolution is that the ability to plug into a world-wide web of unregulated and uncensored digitized information will empower the individual against the institutions – economic, social and political – that control our lives. If the ideal became reality, we would find the individual interacting with the computer in total isolation from our crumbling communities. Anarchic rather than democratic, the ordered rule of the majority would be replaced by the freedom of the jungle. Those, including librarians, who are most blinkered in their pursuit of the all-electronic future seem to believe that because it can be done it will be done – indeed, that in some strange way it has already happened and that libraries and the systematic approach to knowledge and information they provide are already living on borrowed time.

Communicating information

Sending signals down a wire is not providing information, any more than is putting a book on a library shelf or hanging the local train timetables on the station wall. Information is the result of the application of human understanding and interpretation to the transmitted communication. Until that happens, until the digitized information is actually processed by the human brain, it lies as stagnant as an unread journal article or a video collecting dust on a shelf. The generation of electronic data is not of more use, or more value, because it is in electronic form; indeed at the present time it is of less immediate value because comparatively few people have access to the hardware and software which are the essential means of interaction with the data. Heinz von Foerster makes the point:

> What is travelling on that wire, however, is not information, but signals. Nevertheless, since we think we know what information is, we believe we can compress it, process it, chop it up. We believe information can even be stored and then, later on, retrieved: witness the library, which is commonly regarded as an information storage and retrieval system. In this, however, we are mistaken. A library may store books, microfiches, documents, films, slides, and catalogues, but it cannot store information. One can turn a library upside down: no information will come

out. The only way one can obtain information from a library is to look
at those books, microfiches, documents, slides, etc.'[3]

The fact that a record of human knowledge is not available in electronic form does not mean that it is of no use until it is. Our collections of books and other media are words, pictures and sounds
put together by the human mind, which is able to make connec-
tions and links in a way far beyond the limits of mere machine-pro-
cessing. Books have a logical structure of chapters and paragraphs;
they have indexes which take the user down to an intellectually
created and controlled subject level which exceeds, in terms of
quality of analysis, anything which hypertext can provide. Much
more importantly, holding a text in the hand and browsing through
it raises questions the reader would never have thought to ask in
advance. Hypertext links and keyword searches undermine the
intellectual, narrative thread which an author has built in to a book
and which demands sustained reading – a near impossibility on a
computer screen, where the displayed information is visually
divorced from what precedes and follows it. A book is far greater
than the sum of its words. Creative original thought, which pushes
forward the frontiers of knowledge for the individual and for society, depends not on the planned but the accidental encounter with
information.

It is of course the case that some collections exist, not for the primary purpose of enhancing knowledge, but for the provision of
hard facts and information. There is little in common between the
public library, which is still largely book-based and likely to remain
so, and the information units in large corporate and commercial
institutions, where the accent is already on online searching for
speed and currency and where the concept of the virtual library
comes closest to fruition. Those sectors where there is a need for
immediate information have moved over almost wholesale to electronic delivery systems, and it is right and proper that this should
be the case. It is also possible to draw a distinction between the
needs of the old, research-oriented university libraries and those of
the new, applied and teaching-oriented former polytechnics, but
here the distinction is one of degree, not of kind. There are a num-

----

ber of very real, very obstinate reasons why the virtual library will never exist apart from supplying those services (usually entirely commercially based) where currency and speed of access to data are the primary and overriding requirements. The first of those obstinate reasons is the importance of the library with walls to the community it serves.

The importance of environment

'There's no reason why people should have to travel to a library,' says Mr Hammond. 'Within 10 years, I would like to see us giving users the choice of receiving the information and documents they want electronically.' His vision includes dial-up access to the library's databases (including comprehensive information on local and national government and EU services), perhaps from rural cottages, village shops, schools or direct from people's own homes. The local cable company, Norwich Cablevision, is a partner in the virtual library proposals.[4]

So said the Norfolk County Librarian following a disastrous fire which destroyed Norwich Central Library in August 1994. The newspaper article in which his comments appear recycles some of the myths of the virtual library – above all the silent elision of the monumental difference between online access to the listings of the holdings of a collection and online access to the actual content of the collection itself. Many of these myths are nothing but solutions searching for a problem, and first amongst equals is the suggestion that having to actually visit a library knocks the notion of freedom of access into a cocked hat.

There is no evidence whatsoever to suggest that librarians are currently faced with hordes of information-hungry readers anxiously awaiting their next information fix and begrudging the fact that they have had to venture away from their computer screens to get it. For most users of the library, the visit is an enjoyable, social experience and for many it is part of the shared ritual of the life of the community which the library serves. Once again, this is not to suggest that there are not collections whose users do require information on demand, and those collections will naturally be held and accessed in the way which most conveniently answers that demand. That said, all but the most specialized, data-based libraries gain enormously from the physical building that houses their collections, and those gains are practical and psychological for both the individual and for the community.

For, indeed, the library with walls serves both the individual and the community. 'How incredibly perfect it is, in this market-driven society, that from that central spot the great Research Library of the New York Public Library shows the world the significance, substance, and importance of libraries. How crucial it is that it declares to the world that in our democracy there are . . . great . . . collections created for all the people . . .' writes John N. Berry in an editorial supporting the continued construction of libraries in the centre of cities.[5] Not all collections can rival those of the great city and academic centres, of course, but even a small local branch library symbolizes the importance and value which its user community places on the personal development of the individuals which form it. Visiting the library is a public affirmation on the part of the individual of his or her support for the library and its values. In a real sense he or she is participating in those values, in the same way that a voter going to the polls is publicly participating in the democratic process. Sociologists have looked closely at the reasons why people vote, and the 'feelgood factor' which comes from participation in a communally valued process is high on the list.

The 'Information Age', which places so much emphasis on individual interaction with electronic information, has paradoxically brought us the cybercafé, where people meet to talk, drink coffee and use and discover the multitude of facilities available on the Internet. In one of the first examples of the breed to be found in the United Kingdom, the cybercafé is housed in an area lined with books. Some entrepreneurs at least have discovered that not only is information-seeking for leisure purposes a more pleasant activity when carried out in the company of others, but also that books in themselves create a calm, peaceful, secure environment. Surely it would be inconceivable for libraries willingly to abandon circum-

---

stances which are so conducive to fulfilling their objectives and which are one of their greatest assets?

Similarly, when they first entered the United States market, the booksellers Waterstone's quickly discovered that they had to adopt three of their North American rivals' most successful sales tactics – coffee, music and conversation – if they wanted to really bring in the customers. The introduction of a 40-seat café in their new Chicago store led to a marked increase in traffic. While libraries rush to the cold embrace of the virtual library, others in the hard-headed world of business have seen that people need people. Access to electronic information within a physical environment which contains a variety of information sources in a variety of media, each best-fitting different user needs, gives the best of all possible worlds. Librarians have known and understood this for years and must not lose sight of that reality.

What libraries do

The provision of information is only one of the responsibilities of the library, and the way in which the library provides information has always been handled in a different way from that in which it provides access to knowledge. It will be one of the tasks of this book to analyse why this is so, and to discover whether there are ways in which a greater degree of synthesis can be achieved between the two. The printed word is increasingly dismissed as an ineffective means for the rapid distribution of information, but if the book is dead, the corpse is looking remarkably good on it. Publishing flourishes as never before, using the benefits of technology in the production process, indeed, but still producing an artefact which admirably fulfils its purpose.

Of course, books have rarely if ever been the most effective means for the dissemination of time-critical information. Books are the linear expression of organized thought, the expression of a sustained argument, not an accumulation of discrete facts and information. Those books which are so – for example works of reference, encyclopaedias, indexes and abstracts, and directories – have always found a place on library shelves, but as a part of the service the library provides, not the whole. There is now without doubt information that is more effectively transmitted and accessed by electronic means. This is likely to be factual information, or data, which must be current to fulfil the requirements of its recipients. A demand for currency and speed usually points to an underlying commercial value for such data, and as such it is valid to charge for its supply. It would be a false and illogical step for librarians to draw from a single specialized, market-led requirement the conclusion that all information is most effectively held and accessed in electronic form, and that all users want information by electronic means. It would also be wrong to conclude that all users are willing to pay for it at the point of use. Oscar Handin in an article in *American scholar* says: 'Libraries . . . no longer hold a monopoly on information; a flourishing industry now makes such data available through numerous alternative channels . . . The library may not be able to compete in this market, and in any case, the effort to do so may divert attention from what it alone can provide – access to its collections.'[6]

Handin has gone to the heart of the matter. Libraries do far more than provide facts and information; that is one of their purposes, but not the only one, and certainly not one over which they have ever held a monopoly. Libraries provide access to the contents of a collection in an organized and systematic way. The collection consists of what we might call pre-processed knowledge and information, that is, it has been analysed and manipulated into logical patterns through the operation of human thought and intelligence. The collection consists of books which contain linear text for sustained reading; abstracts, indexes and reference works which present organized information; videos which tell a story in pictures; tapes which present combinations of voice and music. The items in a collection are not only the organized output of human endeavour: the library also records and arranges these items in such a way as to give a further structural and organizational layer, which adds value to the whole and makes it far greater than the sum of its parts. This is a very long way from the mere provision of information and is at the heart of the professional values of the cataloguer.

E is for . . . electronic ecstasy

Even in a deregulated market, it is doubtful whether the unfettered laws of supply and demand will inevitably lead to full-scale digitization of existing non-electronic media and a massive shift towards new material being published primarily in electronic form. On the wilder shores of speculation, an editorial by Brian Alley in *Technicalities* trumpets the entry of the Online Computer Library Center (OCLC) into the field of electronic journals. Alley sees the online reference service as providing

> . . . access to users in homes, dorms, offices, and libraries the world over. That's the way in which we will retrieve citations, portions, and full text of what is now starting out at three titles and will expand by the addition of thirty-two more. And that's just the tip of the iceberg . . . By the year 2000, OCLC could easily become the electronic library's drug of choice, supplying thousands of titles to clients everywhere.[7]

Alley gives librarians some equally appealing news as to the price we will pay for such a splendid resource. Waving aside the cost of supply of this drug of choice, he compares the 'possibility of an almost unlimited serials library with virtually no space requirements beyond the terminals it takes to access it' with the cost of maintaining our present serial collections – the cost of new buildings, extensive microfilm collections, binding, adding shelving, and 'millions of hours of expensive and tedious labour devoted to supporting collections'. No wonder administrators love the idea of the electronic library! If we look at some actual figures to offset the hyperbole, we find that in 1991 there were 27 electronic journals, growing to 45 in 1993. Hardly spectacular when set against the 48,000 print serial titles which the British Library Document Supply Centre acquires each year. There will undoubtedly be many more electronic journals in the future – serials are, in many ways, a natural for electronic storage and delivery – but there are factors which will inhibit the growth rates forecast by Alley.

It has been estimated that about 90% of the revenues received from a specialist research journal will be from subscriptions taken out by the specialist library sector. Publishers are inordinately dependent on library subscriptions, but the money available for those subscriptions is being squeezed as libraries everywhere face cuts in their budgets. In the United Kingdom, the proportion of a campus budget spent on library services has fallen from 4% to under 3% in the last decade. This has led libraries to turn to inter-library loan and document supply services – the answer is not to buy just in case, but to supply just in time. Access to a remote source of electronic documents takes the concept of interlibrary loan and document supply and pushes it one stage further. Librarians may fantasize about the mushrooming availability of quality electronic journals for free, but the publishers are going to cling very tightly indeed to their assets – witness the war they have waged against existing document supply services.

Publishers also worry that they will not control the distribution of the electronic product. 'Publishers will not invest in electronic publishing unless they are assured that their work will not be lost through copying. It is not worth spending millions developing a directory if a competitor can copy it perfectly using electronic methods . . .' says Peter Davis, the co-chairman of Reed Elsevier.[8] There are ongoing attempts in the European Union countries to address the problem of copyright of electronic materials. Drawing attention to the problem of tracking data released on to the Internet, and the lack of compensation received by the publishers from the availability of their material to thousands of users, the Copyright in Transmitted Electronic Documents project (CITED) has come up with a model of protection for digital data which is equally applicable to text, images and sound and which will ensure maximum protection and remuneration for information which is routed within CITED-protected systems. The project is at an end, however, and the model may never make the move off the draw-ing board and into the real world. A successor project, Copyright Ownership Protection in Computer Assisted Training (COPICAT) is considering copyright protection of electronic data used in dis-tance learning. There is no hard evidence that the question of copy-right is anywhere near resolution. It undoubtedly will be resolved in time, but at the cost of any semblance of free provision to libraries of copyright protected material.

New copyright or license-to-use restrictions are springing up for reference material which was previously available in book form and bought by the library on a once-and-for-all basis. Publication of this same information on CD-ROM, or its availability through an online service, often requires the library to pay for a license-to-use which may also impose restrictions on who should have access to the material. Increasing the ability to access resources remotely brings with it new policy dilemmas. If the distinction between local and remote users of the library is eliminated, which group should have priority? Which remote users should have access – anybody and everybody? What about electronic resources or data which, for whatever reason, should be accessible only to certain individuals or groups? Many of the larger File Transfer Protocol (FTP) sites storing electronic materials are now so heavily used that 'mirror' sites have been provided to duplicate the resources, and remote users are asked to log on to the smaller academic FTP sites outside peak hours. *CompuServe magazine*, in an article introducing users of its online information service to FTP, warned: 'When you use FTP, the speed of the download will depend on several factors, including how busy the site is at the moment and how quickly network traffic can reach it. Increasing congestion on the Internet has slowed many file operations, while bandwidth – the size of the data channel – depends on how that site sets up its own connection to the Internet. Don't be surprised to see considerable variation in download times.'[9]

Cold turkey

The easy, accessible and free virtual library starts to take on a rather sickly cast when viewed in the cold light of reality. Who pays to digitize the resources? Who pays the phone bill to log on, find, and then download the data? Who pays to put the downloaded data into a form which makes it usable? Once again, we become aware that the new media can limit rather than enhance access to the intellectual content of a work. Electronic resources should be selected on the same rigorous basis as acquisitions in any other medium. What is the library going to forgo to purchase an expensive online resource, and what are the implications for our professional values and objectives if that resource benefits only one sector of the library's clientele?

The amount of book-level material currently in electronic form is infinitesimal. It will grow, but for the great mass of extant material conversion to digital form is highly unlikely. This is not due to problems of copyright or distribution, although such difficulties partly explain the existence of otherwise inexplicable projects such as Project Gutenberg, which aims to put classical, out-of-copyright texts into electronic form – texts which are now available at £1 a copy in any bookshop in a portable, readable format which doesn't require batteries. The one insurmountable obstacle to putting book-level works into electronic form for anything other than purposes of transmission is apparent to anyone who has attempted to read a document more than a few paragraphs in length directly from a computer screen. It is an unpleasant and unsatisfactory experience, physically and mentally. In their book *Future libraries*, Walt Crawford and Michael Gorman have done librarians an inestimable service in presenting the technical evidence for this single, critical fact in a well-documented and incontrovertible form.[10] There is no possibility of computers being used for the kind of sustained reading required to follow a narrative or a reasoned argument. Computer screens are excellent for displaying unconnected pieces of information, but the inability of the user to glance at what precedes and what follows the text displayed on the screen – much less the ability to see what happens several 'pages' away – is a serious hindrance, as is the impossibility of adopting a relaxed posture or reading 'on the fly'. With this in mind, any general library which chooses to go down the path of providing leisure or research textual materials in electronic form must do so on the understanding that readers will find these next to impossible to absorb intellectually. The library will be obliged either to ignore this fact, or to provide a hard copy at the time of use. The first option would be an act of gross unprofessionalism, the second of gross environmental and economic vandalism.

Plus ça change...

In an article titled 'The virtual library: an agenda for the 1990s',[11] Maurice Mitchell and Laverna M. Saunders offer a good example of the school of thought which simultaneously discounts all means of communication previous to the electronic and all the inconvenient, stubborn barriers which will prevent the virtual library ever replacing the real live version. They tell us: 'With the wealth of information now available to students, the teacher no longer can control the information a student sees. Thus the role of the faculty member is shifting from conduit of information to moderator of information and its application.' This is uncritical technophoria indeed. There never was a time when students received only information which had passed through the medium of an authority figure, and the very existence of libraries is one of the proofs of this fact. Then: 'Library budgets still reflect the old days when libraries were funded to provide in-house services to local collections. As budgets fail to keep pace with the volume of information available, the issue of access versus ownership will intensify.' It is a very long time since libraries operated entirely in isolation from one another, as witnessed by extensive interlibrary lending, collection development and cataloguing programmes.

At the same time, the locally held collection is, and will remain, the vital foundation for the organized provision of information and knowledge for a community. To even debate 'access versus ownership' in the context of electronic documents perpetuates the fallacy that access to electronic resources is an alternative to spending money on acquisitions for the local collection. Providing access to electronic resources involves heavy and continuing expenditure on hardware and the telecommunications infrastructure, renewal, upgrades and maintenance, recurrent expenditure on licences to provide access to specific resources and databases, technical support staff, and training in the use of systems which may not be standard. It would seem at the least bizarre to contemplate abandoning collections of organized knowledge and information which have been built over the years, together with the apparatus of catalogues and classification which allow systematic access to that collection –

all for the sake of resources of unknown quality, of more limited coverage, tied to specific hardware and software to enable them to function and, as we have seen which are far from free. Real libraries come ready for use, but they did not get that way quickly or easily. Librarians should not undervalue or undersell the skills that are required to provide and exploit their organized collections, but first they must renew and reaffirm their understanding of the principles underpinning that organizational structure.

It sometimes seems that the more we use computers, the more we are prepared to grant them powers exceeding our own. The real irony underlying their love affair with all things electronic is that librarians – suffering endless angst over their image, ever ready to believe they are out-of-touch, out-of-date, book-loving rejects in need of a life – should become enamoured of a world largely peopled by virtual anoraks – born-again pedants who actually enjoy the mystique and closed world of the Internet. Having indulged in self-flagellation for years over the supposed impenetrable nature of our catalogues and our classification schemes – how dare we impose such arcane mysteries on our users? – we apparently give scarce a passing glance at the difficulties of discovering a Uniform Resource Locator (URL), much less the impossibilities of recalling and transcribing this string of letters and punctuation accurately.

A dead-end profession?

Many librarians believe that information technology has radically altered the library profession, and that the burgeoning electronic online services mean we will have to completely rethink our perceptions of what a library is and the role of librarians in this new setting. Librarians are told that they have a bright future in the 'Information Age' if only they will adopt the role of information brokers. Some may see the role of information technology in libraries as a case of the tail wagging the dog. Nonetheless, this idea of the librarian as information broker follows logically from moves over the last 20 years to rename librarianship as information science and libraries as information centres.

In his book *The myth of the electronic library*, William F. Birdsall has placed librarianship in the 'people centred' professions, together with other public service professionals such as teachers and social workers. In contrast to the doctor or lawyer, who is paid to apply specialist knowledge, the aim of such professionals is to help the clients to help themselves. The librarian can also be seen as working to achieve a social result, by assisting the individual in achieving his or her aspirations and enhancing the good of the wider community in so doing. In many ways cataloguers have a foot in both camps: they are the repository of specialist skills and knowledge which they are paid to apply, but the results of the application of their skills – the catalogue and the classified collection – work together to enable the patron to use the resources of the collection more effectively.

Birdsall sees such public service professionals as librarians as requiring an institutional base: 'The professional authority librarians have derives, then, not from the monopolization of a body of scientific knowledge and its application by a solo practitioner, but from their control of a bureaucratic organization having the power to distribute a public good.'[12] If this is true, we can see that a concept such as the virtual library, far from enhancing the status of librarians, will remove the institutional basis from which they gain their public recognition and which legitimizes their professional skills.

Good public service management is a complex business and of necessity must interpret the inherent professional values of the service within the constraints of the current political and economic environment. Some mixing of the commercial and public service value systems has been possible, but the more common result of mixing the two is a corruption of each. Library managers do not manage their libraries to achieve a growth in profits, but a social result. That social result will differ from library to library, depending on the values of its user constituency. Library managers must balance the key tensions of increasing cost-effectiveness on the one hand, and improving social results on the other. Libraries need to define effective measures of social result, not only to use in the never-ending war to secure funding, but also to focus and motivate staff. Once staff understand the result they are working to achieve, and have agreed measures for that result, the means by which the library collection is managed, developed and used are much less likely to fall prey to every passing technological fancy which offers the promise of more for less.

Investing in our future

Society has to come to a more equitable balance between rights and responsibilities. Those things which the individuals in society agree may be claimed as a right, the individuals in society must take the responsibility to provide. Librarians accept the communitarian values, they embrace the right of free access to information and knowledge, and they also accept responsibility for ensuring provision of that right on behalf of the wider community. If we contract-out the provision of information, we are abnegating that responsibility.

Librarians are committed to the fundamental social result of the self-fulfilment of the individual. It is my contention that to achieve self-fulfilment the individual needs the support of the community, through the provision of publicly funded means for enhancing the public good. Libraries offer a community-based store of knowledge which serves as both communal memory and symbol of the communal present. For each individual, the library offers entry to wider experience and values through these communal resources. Libraries are diverse, serving a multitude of users with an infinity of needs.

In our changing and fractured society, the electronic library presents a mirage of salvation for our hard-pressed services. For librarianship, it is perhaps the ultimate expression of the trends of social fragmentation, economic globalization and the dominance of the market. It is also the idea upon which librarians, in a mixture of panic and despair, have seized as the answer to falling budgets and attacks on professional cohesion. The electronic library will be a library for free – no storage costs, no acquisition costs, no building to heat and light. Masquerading as an enhancement of the right of the individual to information, the electronic library would be, effectively, the privatization of information and the abandonment of the responsibility of the library and librarians to develop the individual in society by the common provision of materials to educate, inform and entertain.

To present a single model for the future library, especially when the model is that of the electronic library, is irrational and simplistic and ignores the economic, social and cultural realities of the real world. The answer to the question of what our libraries will become is not simple. They have always consisted of a mix of media of communication and will continue to do so – print, sound, video, CD-ROM, online: the balance of the mix will differ according to the user community served, but a mix there will be and should be. The job of the librarian is to hold on tight to his or her professional values and to facilitate the exploitation of the content of the library collection, regardless of the medium in which that content is held. How do we communicate to our user communities the vast range and depth of information in our library collections?

References

1 Hutton, Will, *The state we're in*, London, Jonathan Cape, 1995, 15.
2 Penland, Patrick R., *Advisory counseling for librarians*, Pittsburgh, University of Pittsburgh, 1969, 25.
3 Foerster, Heinz von, 'Epistemology of communication', in *The myths of information*, Madison, Wis., Coda Press, 1980, 19.
4 *Independent*, 'A phoenix rises and heads for cyberspace', 13 February 1995.
5 Berry, John N., 'The central library – beyond symbolism', *Library journal*, 1 June 1990, 7.
6 Handin, Oscar, 'Libraries and learning', *American scholar*, 56 (Spring 1987), 213.
7 Alley, Brian, 'OCLC: a source of inspiration. Since when?', *Technicalities*, 14 (12), December 1994, 1.
8 Davis, Peter, 'A European framework for the new media', *Bookseller*, 19 November 1993, 22–4.
9 'Discovering FTP', *CompuServe magazine*, March 1995, 27.
10 Crawford, Walt and Gorman, Michael, *Future libraries*, Chicago, American Library Association, 1995, 17–24.
11 Mitchell, Maurice and Saunders, Laverna M., 'The virtual library', *Computers in libraries*, April 1991, 8–11.
12 Birdsall, William F., *The myth of the electronic library*, Westport, Conn., Greenwood Press, 1994, 98.

CHAPTER 2
ORGANIZING FOR ACCESS

Knowledge empowers an individual and a community, but knowledge in itself does not empower. The individual must provide the will, and the community the ability, to use knowledge. Such is the power of knowledge that those institutions which enable its communication are often viewed with suspicion and hostility. Much more dangerous to democratic societies, however, is the ignorance which inhibits social progress and fosters that suspicion. Democratic societies on the Western model tend to applaud 'information', which is controllable and measurable, but talk little of 'knowledge', which is neither of these things and therefore not an easily marketable commodity. The distinction between the two is important. Libraries, as we have seen, seek to advance knowledge and social development, but they are increasingly distracted from this objective by the parallel pressures of a market-driven environment and the 'information' explosion.

We do not know how much we do not know. Information in electronic form, delivered by electronic means, extends but cannot and should not replace other forms and means of communicated information on the road to knowledge – of all the media it is the most transient and susceptible to change. The seeking of information in the cold isolation of the electronic media, taken together with the limitation of library acquisitions and subscriptions to those items which are requested and used – those for which there is a 'market' – is a lethal combination which is destroying the ability of an individual and community to seek out the new and to think the unthought.

Libraries are based on the values of the community they serve. They represent the agreement of the individuals in a community to communally provide, at communal expense, materials which will be freely available to each individual in the community at the point of use. There are constant attempts to make the library responsive only to the laws of supply and demand – if there is no market for it, don't buy it. Cuts in funding lead to cancellation of periodical subscriptions, and the titles which are cut are those which do not meet acceptable usage targets. Ideas such as 'print on demand', which underlie the concept of the electronic library, are another expression of the dominance of market theory. Policies like the remote supply of low-use items, print on demand and retention based on usage are all sensible attempts to provide information within the context of a market economy, but they are short-term answers which may be undermining the long-term intellectual health of the community.

The new technologies are raising many questions about equality of access to information and knowledge. Using a book, a work of art, a film or a sound recording all involve choice on the part of the user at the level of a single product or work. A price may be involved, but the buyer makes the choice as to what is actually purchased. Broadcast media, on the other hand, involve the purchase of a service – buyers have little control over the specific content of what they receive for their money. In this sense, the online information services are equivalent to the broadcast media. They are a 'world of information' which will – in some inexplicable way – be imbibed by the subscriber with no apparent effort on their part, making them a better, richer person. They are the intellectual equivalent of the no-exercise diet. As with any collection of information, the contents of an electronic database can indeed feed the mind and encourage intellectual growth but, unlike the systematically organized library, which as part of a social contract organizes and records its collection to maximize access to its contents and benefit to its community, the commercial electronic information service has responsibilities extending no further than the satisfaction of users to a level sufficient to retain their subscriptions. Its contract is a financial one with an individual; that of the library is a social one with a community.

The example of the cybercafé has shown us that access to electronic materials by electronic means, in a communal setting which

---

also provides other forms of material accessed through other means, offers the optimum atmosphere for the communication of knowledge and information. Whether it is provided on site or from a remote source, the function of the library is to get information to the user who needs it. How does the user, or the librarian acting as broker for the user, find a potential source for requested information? How do we gain access to the information and knowledge available in and through the library?

Shopping around

People visit libraries in search of food for the mind in much the same way they visit a supermarket in search of food for the body. On most trips, shoppers have a very precise knowledge of what they want – a shopping list of specific items. They know exactly where these items are to be found on the supermarket shelves, they know their approximate price and their quality and have found these acceptable for their purpose. The physical layout of the store, the categorization and secondary categorization of products according to visually perceptible principles, assists in the rapid location of the required items and a successful shopping expedition. Less frequently, shoppers will need to see what is available in the store. They may want a particular product, but have no particular brand in mind. They may be shopping for something they have never previously had occasion to use, and which the supermarket may not stock. Their likely first strategy will be to browse the shelves. If they find something which matches their general requirements, they will be satisfied. If they don't, they may take the trouble to ask a shop assistant for advice. They are more likely to accept something which is available, but doesn't quite meet their needs, than wait until what would be a more suitable option is in stock.

These two shopping experiences exactly match the two types of searches that libraries are organized to assist – specific information searches, and looser searches where the user really needs to discover what is available before making a choice. The user may have nothing as specific as a single item in mind, perhaps only a hazy idea of what he or she wants to know 'about', or may require the answer to a highly specific question which is unlikely to have been written about at the book level. There is, of course, a third type of library user – the impulse reader. It is how we cater for the impulse reader that will ultimately determine the kind of community we produce and the extent to which the library enriches that community.

How do library users find out about the collection? If the library is small, browsing the shelves will usually suffice, or they may prefer to scan a listing, or catalogue, of the items available. For a small collection the order in which this list is presented, or the way in which the items are described, is immaterial and neither enhances nor diminishes the use of the collection. Once the collection reaches even modest proportions, however, a number of options open up. Experience shows that users approach the collection asking either 'Have you got this item?', or, 'Have you got anything on this subject?'. The information needed to answer the first question is perhaps the name of a person associated with the item or a few words from its title. Answering the second depends on the library having organized either the items themselves, or the listing of them, into appropriate groupings of records or items.

Organizing libraries, organizing knowledge

In the same way that the members of the virtual communities on the Internet seek to avoid the usual costs of community membership in the real world, so the protagonists of the virtual library seek to avoid the costs of the real library. They believe that in the virtual library individuals will have free and unrestricted access to 'information', without the controlling hand of the librarian deciding what they find and how they come across it. In fact the hand of the librarian and the professional techniques used to organize knowledge and information liberate the contents of the collection for the communities they serve.

Picture yourself as a novice seeker after information, placed in two situations. In the first, you sit down at a computer to find information 'on the Internet', and in the second you walk into a library. How do you discover what's available?

In the case of the library, the answer is to take a look around. You're not paying connection charges, and can afford to take as long as you like to get your bearings. It is immediately apparent that the materials are organized: books are in subject groupings on the shelves; compact discs and videos are likely to be placed together and may also be categorized in some way according to their content. Within the principal groupings, there is a further level of organization, usually based on some alphabetical or chronological principle. The most important aspect of the organizational structure of the library is that it is visible, it is logical, and it is quickly comprehensible.

In comparison, the user of the Internet is seriously disadvantaged. It is not only that – despite the hype – the information held in electronic form is infinitely less abundant than that available, either physically on-site or by remote access, at a local library. Much more importantly, what is available is organized extremely primitively. There are no visual clues to point you quickly in the right direction, and there is no possibility of taking intellectual shortcuts to get you where you want to be. Michael Gorman has made the point that the Internet is like a 'huge used bookstore (or dare one say library?) in which all the books have been piled higgledy-piggledy having been wrenched from their bindings and having their indexes and front matter removed'.[1] The real library, on the other hand, is organized through a multiplicity of layered and interconnected systems.

The layout of the library resources themselves should assist the user in finding pathways to knowledge. The traditional way in which libraries have organized their collections and their catalogues is to present the records in the catalogue in author order and the books on the shelves in subject order. These two cuts of the intellectual content of the collection interact with each other, as we shall discover later, enabling a multiplicity of means of access depending on the requirements of the user. This traditional structure had been compromised, however, well before the cataloguing of and provision of access to electronic materials became an issue. Items began to be acquired which were – for one reason or another – not interfiled with books on the shelves.

Knowledge records which cannot be interfiled with books, such as videos, audio tapes, slides, photographs, and electronic databases and services, present a difficulty. They usually require specific hardware or software to utilize them, and are probably most effectively grouped together by medium. Given the inclusion of materials other than books in a library, the primary division of the collection is now clearly by format or medium. Within the physical grouping of each form of knowledge record – video, audio tape, disc, book – secondary division is by the most sought characteristic of the intellectual content. We can see this natural principle of organization in practice not just in libraries, but also in bookshops, video stores and even in our own personal multimedia collections. The two basic approaches to the organization of the intellectual content of the collection – by author or title and by subject – persist, regardless of the medium in which it is conveyed, because evidently that is the way the human mind operates.

The development of new media has enabled us to see more clearly the interplay between organizing for access to a physical item and organizing for access to the intellectual content of the item. For the searcher who is approaching the collection by anything other than its primary division, the catalogue and the classification scheme work together to provide a rich diversity of approaches and ensure the effective utilization of the contents of the collection. The primary cut of the physical collection is by medium; the primary cut of the intellectual collection is by author and title and by subject.

As universities built their collections they naturally chose to organize on the basis of their system of instruction – a return to a rough-and-ready subject approach to the physical location of material. Classification systems such as the Dewey Decimal Classification and the Library of Congress Classification were also based on the academic disciplines. Two classificatory approaches can be discerned: a practical approach, based on the requirements of the user community and designed to enhance access to and use of the collection; and a theoretical approach which attempted to organize knowledge itself on the basis of scientific principles. It was not the quantitative growth of information and knowledge alone which came to present problems for the classification schemes which developed in the 19th century, but also the development of new branches of knowledge which overlapped and redefined the long-standing disciplinary boundaries.

In British libraries at least, the classification scheme fulfilled a dual role. It served as a means of arranging items in a linear sequence on the basis of their principal subject content, and, in the classified catalogue, it served to group together the catalogue records for all works dealing with a particular subject, regardless of whether this was the primary subject of the item. The classified catalogue presented the collection from the point of view of the systematic organization of knowledge employed by the classification scheme.

The 19th century marked the development and culmination of approaches to information organization which are still dominant today. The catalogue and the collection were inextricably bound. Within the world of each individual library, the catalogue had to serve the fundamental purpose of providing access to the collection. It was a finding list – a brief description of the item, together with a device indicating its location on the shelves. Anthony Panizzi, the Keeper of Printed Books at the British Museum Library and the driving force behind the first published British Museum Catalogue, used authorship as the governing principle for the catalogue, and indeed did not believe in subject classification for libraries. In the closed access world of the British Museum Library this was an understandable and acceptable point of view, but the lack of a coherent means of subject access to its collection is a problem which haunts the British Library to this day.

In his book *Information access*, Richard Joseph Hyman makes the point that the earliest librarians were more interested in a subject, rather than an author, approach to their collections. 'Only as the Western concept of individualism grew stronger did the need for author identification arise'.[2] Even into the 19th century, individuals were often identified by a name which included a patronymic, a place of origin, or the trade of the individual rather than the label of forename and surname. In this very early example, we see the way in which individualism is in creative tension with a collective approach to the organization of information, enhancing and focus-

---

ing attention on known item searching at the expense of grouping mechanisms for intellectual works.

The catalogue, the classification, and quality access

The principal purpose of the catalogue is to list and describe the items in the collection. It also attempts to tell the user, at the macro level, which intellectual works can be found in the collection, regardless of whether or not these works are carried in discrete physical items. A couple of examples will serve to illustrate the point. The catalogue will tell you that the library holds an item called *The Oxford book of Victorian poetry*. It will not tell you which individual poems, each one a distinct intellectual work in its own right, are to be found in that item. The library may hold the CD *JFK assassination: a visual investigation*. This is a work in its own right; a compilation of video clips, photographic images, maps and computer projections relating to the assassination of John F. Kennedy. It also contains the text of two other distinct works, both also published in book form: the Warren Commission report and *Crossfire: the plot that killed Kennedy* by Jim Marrs. A good catalogue will indicate that the library holds these intellectual works, even though they are not available as discrete physical items and are not in their original book form.

The bibliographic descriptions are systematically organized – that is, their relationship one to another is defined – through the addition of data which functions as a means of access both to the described item and to the intellectual work it carries. An access point is a vocabulary-controlled string of words which forms a unique label for a specific name, title or subject connected with a work. It is important to recognize that a point of access gets you to a bibliographic description, not to the item on the shelves. Access points include: names connected with a work, such as the name of an author, an illustrator, the band performing a song; titles connected with a work – the title by which the intellectual content of an item is commonly known, the title of a series in which a work is issued; and a description of the subject content of a work. The form and structure of the words by which names and titles are represented in access points, as well as the description of the item with which they are connected, are governed by descriptive cataloguing rules; the subject access points are generated by the application of the rules of a subject indexing scheme to the results of subject analysis.

The strategies which users pursue in order to find information are strongly affected by the structure of the tool they are using to carry out the strategy. The organizational structure of all but the electronic catalogue is readily apparent to the user. If there is no perceptible structure, users can have no other strategy than to keyword search, whether that keyword is a word from a name or a title, or a word which is an attempt to define a subject, until they find something which satisfies them. Keyword searching is a means of access, but it is not a system of access because its results are not predictable. There is a strange perception that if catalogues are enhanced with more and more 'keywords', whether from tables of contents or even from the text itself, then we will somehow get so close to the quality of retrieval provided by systematic access that it will no longer be necessary to invest expensive human resources in creating and allocating those vocabulary-controlled access points. This is not the case.

Classification groups the physical items themselves to provide another means of approaching the intellectual content of the collection. These two systems, the catalogue and the classified collection, work in harmony to provide an interdependent means of organized access to the organized collection. When we get down to the discrete physical item itself, there is the possibility of yet further systematic access through the item's index or contents page. At this level, however, the means of access becomes item specific – that is, access is not dependent on standards applicable across items, such as a classification scheme or a cataloguing code, but on the individual whim of the compiler. The information being indexed is at a level below that of the whole work, and, as we will see in the next chapter, the problems inherent in providing analytical or deep access to the content of the collection are persistent, pervasive and extensive.

Life is simple when you know what you want

Those searches that are simplest for the library to facilitate are the 'known item' searches, in which the catalogue is approached with information relating to a specific item whose existence is known to the searcher. Many forces are driving us towards focusing attention almost exclusively on providing access to known items. The first of these forces is the computer itself, which has made searching infinitely more flexible and powerful than in the past, but which depends on the input of known, item-specific data to demonstrate that power and flexibility. It may be just a couple of words from the title of a film, or a word from the name of the rock band performing the musical work, but if the word appears on the item and if it has been accurately keyed into the computer, then a record of the item will be retrieved. Many other records which contain the same word may be retrieved as well, but the search is answered and the searcher hasn't missed potentially relevant material. Known item searches have a definite answer – the item either is or isn't there – and this quantifiable, measurable result is very appealing to library administrators looking for easily demonstrable performance measures to support their search for funding.

If the computer can work these wonders for us, why do we need to employ anything other than good copy typists to record data as it appears on the item? The question is not new: the answer is the same now as it has always been. If all requests were for known items – 'known' in the sense that the searcher accurately recalls some data appearing on the physical item or items required – then cataloguers and cataloguing rules would not be necessary. The catalogue answers far more complex and stimulating questions than those we have looked at so far.

Isn't it nice to be in control?

The value of the catalogue lies in the fact that it offers a systematic means of access to the collection which is predictable by its users. Access is primarily enabled by the ability to search the catalogue using words connected with the item. If they observe that the catalogue is searchable by name, they learn that searching by a name word will bring results. If they observe that the catalogue is searchable by words from a title, they rapidly conclude that searching by a word describing a subject in which they are interested will bring results, by retrieving records for all items with titles containing that word.

This simple keyword access is fine as far as it goes, but it is immeasurably enriched by the systematic vocabulary control of author, title and subject words. Only through the rigorous application of this vocabulary control can anything close to the totality of systematically recorded information in the collection relating to the sought author, title or subject be retrieved. Delivering this control is an intellectual process, demanding the intuitive leaps and subjective mental links which a machine is not capable of making – although machines are very good at maintaining the intellectual system once it is in place.

Accurate and comprehensive grouping for enhanced access requires the unique identification of the names, works and subjects appearing in the catalogue. Most communication services involve the establishment of some form of unique identification data to enable them to function. A telephone directory, for example, is a listing of names, but each individual name does not have to be a unique string of data. The allocation of a unique telephone number to an individual location is the principal component in a voice communication system. An individual's e-mail address, however, has to be unique at the name and location level. The name and location act together to ensure that all messages are delivered to a unique location, in the same way that a unique number ensures connection for the phone system. How do we ensure the grouping at a single location in the catalogue of all names relating to an individual, all titles referring to an intellectual work, and all intellectual works on a distinct subject?

The recording of data critical to the successful completion of searches other than those for known items is an intellectual task carried out according to standard methods of analysis and employing a controlled vocabulary. The process is undertaken by the person creating the catalogue record as a one-off task, which, when correctly completed, ensures that every subsequent search for information related to that name, work or subject will retrieve all records in the catalogue appropriate to the search. Without a vocabulary-controlled subject access point, for example, the only way to get anywhere near comprehensive access to the relevant material which the library possesses would be to search under all of the possible synonyms and variant spellings of the sought subject. Of course this is a hopelessly ambitious task, if only because there is no way of knowing with certainty when it has been completed.

It would be possible to reduce the cost of producing the catalogue record by reducing the amount of time spent in creating and allocating this controlling and structuring access point data, but the catalogue would be substantially reduced in value and the collection would be used much less effectively. Searchers would be able to retrieve records for items of which they had prior knowledge and accurate information regarding the title or other identifying data, but they would not be presented with the catalogue records of additional relevant material in the collection. If the critical search data in a catalogue record has been effectively controlled, access to the information and knowledge contained in the collection is deeper and richer. Each searcher does not have to reconstruct independently the intellectual links in the search chain, but he or she does have to understand the basis of the intellectual decisions taken by the cataloguers creating the catalogue and, most importantly of all, has to know that those decisions have been taken.

Does the catalogue still fulfil this function of pulling together all items relating to a specific author, work or subject? We have seen how the physical organization of items in the collection has impeded collective subject access by separating collections on the basis of medium. A video of the television series 'Absolutely fabulous' is unlikely to be found on the shelves next to the published book of the scripts. The catalogue, however, is in a unique position to pull these items together in a variety of ways, and will do so whether the catalogue medium is card, fiche or computer. Through the addition to the record for each catalogued item of a vocabulary-controlled access point for the intellectual work which that item conveys, a catalogue search brings together two items separated in the physical collection.

A striking example of the power of this systematic, rule-based analysis is that of the film *The madness of King George*. Alan Bennett's original play has the title *The madness of George III* but it was felt that the title had to be changed so that cinema-goers in the United States wouldn't mistakenly assume that they had missed the first two films in the series! A cataloguer faced with a video of the film would first of all have to decide whether the catalogue record should have a uniform title access point – are the film and the stageplay inherently manifestations of the same intellectual work? If so, the uniform title for the intellectual work, added to the descriptions of both discrete items, will bring together the records for the film and the stageplay in a catalogue search. Should the cataloguer decide that the content of the items does not represent the same intellectual work, all is not lost – the catalogue would still bring the existence of the film and the play to the attention of the searcher, by the addition of an access point for a 'related' work to the record for each item.

Small packets of information and data are much more amenable to electronic transmission and access. They are also, of course, much more amenable to organization and indexing. The intellectual challenge in the vocabulary control of names does not lie in deciding the form of words used to define the name, but in ensuring that the same string of words appears on every catalogue record with a primary association with that name. In subject indexing, on the other hand, the challenge is to create the string of words which will most suitably define the subject of the item for the community who will be using the collection.

The catalogue or index may allow for either post-coordinate or pre-coordinate searching. The arguments for and against each of these methods mirror those for and against vocabulary control itself. In a post-coordinate search system, individual subject terms from a controlled vocabulary are allocated to the catalogue record for an item. Users searching on a term will retrieve all the records to which that term has been allocated. In a pre-coordinated system, the individual subject terms are related to each other following the rules of an indexing standard. The first system has the advantage that it is high on recall, but it is also potentially low on relevance; the second system will recall fewer items, but of a potentially greater relevance. Pre-coordinate systems are preferable for searches where the user has a firmer knowledge of the specific subject information he or she is seeking; post-coordinate systems allow more opportunity for the user to decide what is or is not relevant. The sheer number of records retrieved for searches on very general subject terms may deter the searcher from persevering with the search.

In later chapters we will look at the importance of standards in helping to define uniformly the structure and content of a catalogue record, and also at some of the ways in which the standards can more effectively be applied by cataloguers in a time of reduced resources for cataloguing. What is important at this stage is to understand the value of the systematic organization of knowledge in enhancing access.

They don't make catalogues like that any more

The user of a computer catalogue never sees the catalogue as a whole. The records in a computer catalogue have no primary fixed relationship one to another, but are brought together in an infinity of temporary groupings, each of which is generated in response to a question. If the user asks, for example, for a list of the records which include the word 'house' in the title, at the touch of a key there will be presented all the records which fit the bill. At this point, as the records scroll past on the screen, we can no longer avoid the restrictions of the two-dimensional world, and neither should we wish to. The records must follow each other, and they must be displayed according to some prescribed order. This may be chronological, by publication date or by the date the record was added to the catalogue; or alphabetical, by author name or first word of title. Whatever the order, it must be comprehensible to the searcher – especially if the number of records retrieved is more than a screenful.

Computer catalogues give only what they are asked for. They are superbly good at locating specific data rapidly and comprehensively: they are not good for any kind of browsing other than a serendipitous keyword search. It is difficult to pin down why this is the case. 'Physical' catalogues, whether on card or fiche or in print, follow one basic organizational principle. Paradoxically that is limiting but at the same time liberating, once the principle is grasped. The mere fact that the records in a computer catalogue cannot be seen other than a screen at a time, and that the records *en masse* in the database have no intellectual relational principle to each other, makes it difficult to know not only where to go, but also when a search has been completed – or, more importantly, when relevant records have been missed. These are some of the limitations we have already come across in relation to searching electronic databases and texts as a whole.

This lack of a clear perception of the organization of the catalogue is a problem, too, for the people whose job it is to put the catalogue together. Before the advent of the computer catalogue, cataloguers had of necessity to understand the organizational principles on which cataloguing and classification were founded, because those principles defined the way in which the individual catalogue records were placed within a single linear order in a physical catalogue. Now the organizational principles are not made manifest in a physical form. It is true that some of those principles are no longer of relevance in the automated environment, but others continue to be of vital importance in enabling systematic access to the collection.

Although the computer catalogue is well-nigh universal today, users and librarians should beware of forgetting the wealth of organized information available to them outside its confines. Many collections of records for older or specialist materials have not yet been converted to computer-readable form. These card or print catalogues, apart from their coverage of rare or obscure material, are often organized and presented in a way which is of real value in enabling access to their content in response to certain types of research query. An example is the printed *British Library Catalogue*, which makes its primary organizational division by author name, followed by a secondary division which organizes by work under each author name. Within the sequence for each work, the individual item descriptions are then listed chronologically in order of publication. The ability to observe this structure visually, without the limitations of screen-by-screen scrolling or the deluge of unstructured postings resulting from a keyword search on author name or name of the work, is an inestimable advantage. It is next to impossible to analyse and comprehend the results of a computer catalogue search without printing out the results of that search.

Setting aside the question of coverage, we have a second difficulty when searching computer catalogues, and again it is one which is largely disguised from the user because of the nature of the medium itself. Retrospective conversion by and large does not mean recataloguing. To take the *British Library Catalogue* again as an example, the all-important name access points were created in the context of the British Museum cataloguing rules introduced by Panizzi. Although these same name access points are of course still present in the retrospectively converted computer catalogue, if we put the converted *BLC* together with the catalogues for modern material, whose name access points are established to the requirements of the Anglo-American Cataloguing Rules, we end up with a collection of catalogues that are not collectively name vocabulary controlled. A name access point will not necessarily have the same form in each of the catalogues, because different standards were used in structuring that name access point. This means that a user searching across the catalogues using a single name form would not necessarily retrieve all of the records for material in the British Library relevant to his or her search. The computer can do much, but it cannot in itself provide the enhanced quality of access which comes from the intellectual process of rigorous, systematic, vocabulary control.

Knowledge is all

The set-up of a system like a library is much more significant in determining the results of a search than factors such as the skill or expertise of the searcher. People on the whole prefer ease of access to the quality of the information they retrieve. This may be because they have low expectations, or because they are often not really sure what information they want and are therefore unable to assess the value of their search result. Librarians are faced with the challenge of expanding the controlled systems of access they provide through the organization of knowledge, and at the same time making these systems transparent to the user so that they are led, by means of embedded intellectual and machine links, to the information they need. In many ways librarians have succeeded in this task too well. There is the perception amongst many that cataloguing is a mechanical task, and that machines would do it cheaper and quicker.

Talk of rules and systems, the jargon of access points and the organization of knowledge, undoubtedly leads to the reaction that surely, with computers, all this stuff can't still be necessary? Are cataloguers so ingrained in their prehistoric, print-based, linear systems that they can't see the electronic wood for all those paper-producing trees, or is it that they are engaged in an illogical act of self-delusion designed to convince themselves – if nobody else – that they still have a role in today's library? Richard Joseph Hyman has said: 'A basic understanding of the elements of information organization is essential for effective search and retrieval. This understanding is based . . . on recognizing what access points have been provided by the various Anglo-American cataloguing codes, subject authorities, and indexing systems to facilitate . . . searching for the original behind the surrogate.'[3] Hyman is right in his assessment that users (including cataloguers) need an understanding of the elements of information organization to get optimum access to a collection's contents, but it is an understanding of the theory – of how and why information has been organized – that is of importance, rather than a knowledge of the results of the application of the organizational concepts. If a user understands that all works in the collection related to George Gissing have been grouped together in the catalogue under a single label for that name, then wider usage of the collection will be infinitely more fruitful than possession of the factual information that the label consists of the words 'Gissing, George, 1857–1903'. The first line of defence is attack – we must have a clear understanding of the continuing value of our organized systems of access.

References

1   Gorman, Michael, 'Coping with the chaos', *California libraries*, **5** (5), May 1995, 3.

---

2   Hyman, Richard Joseph, *Information access*, Chicago, American
    Library Association, 1989, 2.
3   Hyman, Richard Joseph, *Information access*, Chicago, American
    Library Association, 1989, xi.

CHAPTER 3
DIGGING DEEPER, CASTING WIDER

We have seen how the library systematically organizes its resources so as to enable access to both their physical and intellectual content by the user community. How deep down can we dig into that intellectual content, though? How do we satisfy the user who has discovered the existence of a potentially relevant information source which the library doesn't possess? Information about the collection and its contents is scattered inside and across a host of different resources, many in different formats and media, many needing differing logical 'software' to use.

Mining the collection

For most visitors to the library, browsing will be the principal means by which they discover information. As we have already seen, the physical organization of the resources of the library provides a deeper level of access not available through a catalogue search alone. Browsing a classified collection is a rapid way of finding relevant material, with no prior knowledge of what might be available on the sought subject. Equally valuable is the depth of access possible from location of an item, followed by a search of that item's index. There is a perception that because word-by-word searching is not possible until a text has been digitized, then the intellectual content of an item is not accessible at all. Paradoxically, this is the exact opposite of the truth. We may not yet have many digitized texts – we may never have many digitized texts – but we do have millions of books with indexes. Electronic information often exists in a virtual state of nature: unorganized internally, unrecorded and uncatalogued externally. Book indexes, when used within the context of a classified collection, are the great forgotten means of systematic deep access to the content of an item.

Although contents page data is often seen as providing additional access remote from examination of the item itself, there has been surprisingly little computerization of book indexes.

Given the lack of digitized full texts, and the distinct possibility that these will never exist in large numbers, there is absolutely no other means of obtaining in-depth access to the intellectual content of an item other than to find it and to look at it. This points up the vital role of classification and subject indexing in the scheme of integrated systematic access to a collection. The dominance of computer catalogues means that we have gained on the enhanced access swings, but we have lost on the added conceptual value roundabout. The biggest loser has been classification, which is now perceived by most users, and maybe by most librarians – even in the United Kingdom – as little more than a shelving device giving a rough subject grouping for the benefit of browsers. At the same time the fundamental principle of classification – intellectual subject analysis, the results of which are capable of expression in a single sequence of numbers or letters which is language-independent – seems to have extraordinary potential for use in a computer-based subject access system.

The one-stop information shop – not!

At a level separate from the physical items themselves, the catalogue is the next most obvious means of discovering the content of the collection. We have to say right here and now that the catalogue will not answer all our questions about the collection, but then that never has been its purpose. It may as a minimum requirement list the items in the collection, but this is by no means the same thing as listing all the intellectual works contained within those items – much less the content of each of those intellectual works. For the researcher seeking to identify, locate and obtain information, the challenge is navigation of the diverse sources of access to this collection content. For the librarian, it is creating, maintaining and integrating those various sources of access into a coherent whole. The collection of a library, the distinct intellectual works which it contains, is a vast resource which is only partially charted, and which is still only partially navigable through the systematic organization and presentation of data provided by the cataloguer.

It is usually not possible to know with certainty that an item is useful solely from the record for that item in a catalogue or listing. The catalogue record can give enough clues, though, to suggest whether the item is worth investigating further. The record may show the presence of particular illustrative matter, or contain a classification number and subject headings which indicate that the item is of relevance in answering an information need. Certainly if the catalogue contains vocabulary-controlled access points the searcher will get enhanced quality of access to the collection content. It is only by looking at the item itself, though, that the searcher will be able to come to a true assessment of the worth of the item relative to particular information needs.

Conventionally, catalogue records are prepared for whole bibliographic items – monographs, serials, films, maps, etc. Many of these whole items will consist of or contain more than one bibliographic work. The rules by which descriptive cataloguing is governed allow for the bibliographic analysis of an item, for the express purpose of providing access to such works. The previous chapter used as an example the CD *JFK assassination: a visual investigation*, which contains two works previously published independently in book form – the catalogue should, of course, facilitate access to these two works if the collection is to be exploited efficiently. However, although cataloguing codes such as the Anglo-American Cataloguing Rules certainly enable libraries to provide this systematic analytical cataloguing, very few libraries have the resources to provide anywhere near the full depth of bibliographic analysis in their catalogues. Although the rules enable, library resources deny. This is not the only occasion on which we will discover that something commonly criticized as an omission or restrictive practice in the cataloguing rules is, in fact, the result of library policy on application of the rules.

Whilst it is an undeniable fact that the catalogues of most libraries always have and always will list only a proportion of the intellectual works in their collections, the actual percentage listed is open to debate. In an article in *Technicalities* David Tyckoson has

---

put that percentage at only 2% for a large university library.[1]
Tyckoson believes this is an indication of the failure of the catalogue to fulfil its primary objective at an increasing rate. Figures
such as this are only fuel to the fire of those who argue that traditional library systems and processes are no longer of value in
attempting to record, control and give access to the contents of electronic media.

What is beyond debate is that the librarian has traditionally had
to find ways other than resource-intensive cataloguing to provide
access to hidden intellectual works. One area where analytical
access has almost invariably been provided by other means than
through the catalogue is that of journal articles. In themselves, journal articles do not pose a problem to the catalogue and to the standards and principles by which it is compiled and organized. What
does pose a problem is the sheer volume of this material, particularly for research libraries that not only subscribe to many journals
but whose community user base is research oriented and requires
real depth of access. It has long been apparent that such libraries
are not individually resourced to carry out the indexing task
required of them, and they have turned to the commercial
providers of indexing services. Whilst this has had the positive
effect of relieving pressure on the library's staff resources, it has also
meant that the library has lost independent control over the means
of access – in terms of the 'how' and the 'what' – to an important
part of its collection.

Indexing services can exist in a variety of formats: in print, on
CD-ROM, fiche, and increasingly as part of an online service.
Because libraries have invariably found it impossible to produce
analytical access to their collections unless the community they are
serving is a specialist community willing to fund access at this level,
they have by and large been a captive market for the indexing service providers. The indexing systems used by these services often
do not conform to library standards, or are not applied in conventional ways. This means that not only is access to the indexed material not integrated into the mainstream search and retrieval
mechanism – the catalogue – but also the access provided by the

index may not follow the systematic organizational principles found in other library tools.

Libraries often find that use of an online or CD indexing service is regulated by a license. These licenses define conditions such as how many users can access the resource at the same time, and where these users can be located. The producers of these information resources are by and large commercial organizations which naturally want to get the fullest possible return from their investment, whilst at the same time safeguarding their existing and future user base. The librarian, however, is not entirely without power in this relationship. Producers of electronic information resources, like publishers of printed resources, are often heavily dependent on the library market. Librarians, in this instance, are consumers and should be prepared to use their power to influence the supply side of the information market. Libraries can certainly demand the right to retain out-dated CDs, or to secure online database licenses which reward high volume usage; equally they should support where possible those products which can best be integrated into their standard means of information access and retrieval.

Analytical access to the content of serial literature is provided by commercial indexers outside the context of a specific library collection and a specific user community. In some cases the index will use a general library standard such as Library of Congress Subject Headings, or a custom-built system which nonetheless adopts the same logical approach. Others will provide entries only under keywords from the article title – KWIC and dirty subject access. This is better than nothing and may well be sufficient as a form of current awareness service. Indexes which are provided 'in house' for special collections such as photographs or slides will generally provide a subject approach and terminology based on the specific requirements of the community who will be using the collection. It seems that serial indexes are a point on the bridge spanning the whole bibliographic item approach of the general library catalogue, and the in-depth indexing of its specialist materials. These differing avenues of access are provided and have developed in response to the differing requirements of those setting out on the search for information. You choose the road to take depending on the purpose of the journey and the most important constraints in carrying out the journey.

We would be very unwise to believe that access to the content of a collection has ever been comprehensive and consistent. That is not to say that such a goal is not to be aimed for or that it is not one which can be achieved, to a greater or lesser degree, by a gradualist approach within and between library bibliographic systems. The growth of electronic media and the realization that libraries are not creating access at the analytic level for electronic material does not mean that we must immediately rush to abandon our developed systematic means of access to a variety of media at the whole item level. The electronic medium may be new, but the problem of analytical access most certainly is not. The library has always failed to provide full analytical access to its collections, in whatever medium they are held. It is to resolving that much wider general issue of analytical access that we need to address our attention.

Adding value to access

The wave of enthusiastic journalism lauding the ability of the Internet to provide 'remote access' to a library strangely confuses the catalogue with the collection. Consulting the catalogue of a remote library online is no different in kind from consulting the printed or fiche catalogue of a remote library. Access to the catalogue of a collection is not access to the collection itself, or anywhere near it. Indeed, if Tyckoson's figures are to be believed, this 'remote access' may mean nothing more than being able to log on and discover whether the information we need can be found in the records for the 2% of its material covered by the library catalogue. We have a far more deep-seated problem in delivering access to our collections than can be answered by computer networking alone.

Indexes are traditionally placed together with other reference works in the library. These materials are routes to information which is not to be found in the catalogue, either because it is 'deep' information accessible at the whole item level by means of an item index, contents page, film credits, database listing of files, etc., or, for some of the material referred to or indexed, because it is only accessible at a site remote from the library itself. The key point about all these second level access sources, whatever their medium, is that they should be recorded in the primary level of access to the collection content, the catalogue. The catalogue will group these second level access tools, be they individual books, films or tapes, indexes or encyclopaedias, be they on CD, online databases, or print under the controlled vocabulary labels which it uses for names, subjects and titles. The user is informed of the existence and coverage of these sources through the catalogue. So we see that, although the library catalogue provides a single point of access to neither all of the intellectual content of the collection, nor to universal knowledge and information, it does record and index the materials available to take us one step further down that road. It is not a necessary function of the catalogue to record and index in depth, because that in-depth indexing is already provided elsewhere at the whole bibliographic item level. Those who are calling for cataloguers to 'catalogue the Internet' are misguided: to provide access at anything other than the whole item level has never been the function of the catalogue. That is not to say that the standards we have now are not capable of that task – this point will be discussed further in the next chapter – but we must beware of destroying the fitness of these standards for their purpose in order to make them fulfil an end it has never been the role of the catalogue to provide.

Bewitched, bothered and bewildered

The wider we extend the coverage of vocabulary control across the records of the collection, the further we will extend the frontiers of recall of relevant material. However, as we have seen, the catalogue itself rarely gives access to more than a percentage of the intellectual content of the collection. There are other means of access to works and information hidden at the macro level of the catalogue. Conventionally libraries have contracted-out the provision of access to a high proportion of this material, particularly that falling into certain categories such as journal articles, database contents, and book indexes.

This is a matter of great concern to the librarian who wants to exploit the collection fully . If the potential of the collection is to be maximized, the library user must be provided with as wide a range and variety of access routes as possible to the deep content of the collection, and also to remote information sources to which the library is linked. The catalogue approaches the ideal high-quality access model in providing vocabulary-controlled access, systematically applied. However, the catalogue is biased towards access at the whole bibliographic item level. Analytical access to the content of these whole bibliographic items must be provided by individual or corporate indexing services.

The catalogue covers the whole-item sources available in a discrete physical location. Once the searcher has found an item in the catalogue, there will be a fair chance of obtaining immediate access to that item if it is at the location specified in the catalogue. In searching an index purchased rather than produced by the library, the user encounters two problems that potentially inhibit access: the product will index materials the library does not possess, and there will be materials the library possesses which are not indexed by the product. In the first case the user is frustrated because, having found, for example, a relevant journal article, he or she cannot immediately get hold of the journal in which it appears. In the second case potentially relevant material that is readily accessible is hidden from the user because it does not appear in the index.

Full-text databases present some new problems for librarians seeking to extend systematic access. These databases are huge works of reference, where relevance has been sacrificed to recall and no attempt has been made to assist the user by the imposition of any prior structuring, ordering or sorting of the data other than that which can be carried out by machine. The difficulties and the delights of full-text searching are pointed up in an article by Francis Wheen, who tried out 'the world's most expensive and exclusive computer game'.[2] *The English poetry full-text database* was issued on CD in June 1994 by Chadwyck-Healey Ltd. The intention of the product – retailing at £27,000 – is to provide a single source for every piece of English verse published between AD 600 and 1900.

There are 160,000 poems, by 1,350 authors, on 4 CD-ROMs, plus software and instruction manual:

> And so . . . I found myself gazing at a VDU in the London Library reading room, with the entire canon of pre-20th-century poetry only a keystroke away. Load up the disks and off we go.
>
> But where do we go? The 'search options' are so comprehensive – 'keyword, first line, title keyword, poet name, period' – that I was paralysed with indecision, embarrassed by richness. While brooding on my next move, I tapped in the Prime Minister's surname . . .

The search strategy adopted by Wheen in casually approaching this electronic product was the same as that adopted for any reference tool by a user with no particular goal in mind – look up a word (your own name, if no other springs to mind). Full-text databases are different from other formats in that they can contain an immense amount of material in a small amount of space. The way in which they can be searched is both literal and comprehensive. But these very strengths spawn weaknesses. It is possible to discover how often the word 'robe' appears in a digitized text of *Macbeth* in a nano-second, but it is not possible to discover all of the imagery of ill-fitting clothes present in the play. Their lack of systematic, vocabulary-controlled, interpretative indexing lessens the value of these full-text products for the serious researcher who, for optimum benefit, must continue to use them in conjunction with other access tools and with an intelligent appreciation of their limitations.

The problem of changes in cataloguing codes, particularly when these changes affect vocabulary-controlled access points, should not be minimized and should act as a warning sign of the peril of changes to standards solely for change's sake. In many ways computer catalogues encourage the belief that the form of access points can now be changed at will – if we have the facility for global update of access points across all our catalogue records. But of course, this is to forget the existence of those other forms of access that are not readily susceptible to change or indeed are not under our control to impose change. A ready example is to be found in the way in which cataloguing codes have addressed the question of the form a name is to take when used as a heading in the catalogue. The British Museum code and its successors used the fullest form of the real name as the basis for the access point. There were sensible and logistical reasons for taking this decision in terms of the catalogue forms prevalent in the 19th century. In the first place, if the vocabulary-controlled form was not directly equivalent to the form of name as it appeared in an item, then it did not have to reflect every passing change in the way the name appeared in subsequent items. Secondly, the fullest form was that most likely uniquely to identify an author – a requirement if the catalogue was to assist the searcher by placing together all the works with which a person was connected. Although use of the full name met all the requirements of the library in providing systematic access, its major flaw was that the resulting heading was sometimes far from the name with which a searcher would approach the catalogue. The British Library Catalogue, for example, lists the works of Jack London under 'London (John Griffith)'. The second edition of the Anglo-American Cataloguing Rules enshrined the principle of 'commonly used name' as the starting point for constructing a vocabulary-controlled name access point. There are other instances of differences between codes in their approach to the treatment of compound surnames, or names which include a prefix. The form in which headings for corporate bodies such as government agencies, societies and institutions are to appear in the catalogue is even more fraught with difficulty, particularly when problems of language rear their head. Will the name of a German government agency be found under 'Germany' or under 'Deutschland'?

Subject headings face the additional problem of choice of words to express an often imprecise concept. This is not just a case of deciding the language of the words, or whether a scientific or a popular term should be used. Words have changing meanings over time; they also change in their degree of acceptability to the community. Subject headings have to be responsive to such changes if they are to meet the needs of the communities they serve but, like name headings, they also need to maintain a level of stability to assist searching across a variety of access tools. The most important objective for the providers of vocabulary-controlled subject access is to achieve as near-perfect a match as possible between the words *they* choose to describe the contents of a work, and those likely to be chosen by searchers. Although this may be possible within the context of any one collection and its community of users, difficulties arise once the catalogue record and its subject headings and classification number are taken out of that specific environment and placed in another – or even when the home catalogue is accessed by a remote user. The new environment may utilize a different subject indexing or classification scheme, or the remote user may require a much greater level of subject specificity in deciding whether the item is worth further consideration.

Weaving the access web

These are all issues which relate to enhancing access, rather than providing it; they are indicators of value and quality for the library, and valid targets for librarians to aim at in service provision to their communities. At its simplest level, the catalogue will act as a finding list enabling the identification and retrieval of an item from the collection. However, once the records in the catalogue are taken out of the context of their specific environment and used for remote access – whether by means of publication of the catalogue, or by putting the catalogue on the Internet – the records lose some of their value. Information which identifies an item in a specific physical location does not necessarily answer the questions of a remote user of the record, who has not the option of going and looking at the book to see if it is of relevance. Panizzi recognized that the *British Museum Catalogue of Printed Books* had to be much more than a finding list: it had to function as a national bibliographic reference source, capable of use outside the British Museum, and containing records usable independently of the item they described. Recognizing the importance of consistency in producing such a tool, Panizzi created the 91 Rules according to which records for the items in the BM Department of Printed Books were to be catalogued.

In subsequent moves to make the catalogue more than a finding list, Cutter's *Rules for a dictionary catalog*, first published in 1876, stand as a landmark. He defined the objectives of the catalogue as:

1. To enable a person to find a book of which either (A) the author (B) the title (C) the subject is known
2. To show what the library has (D) by a given author (E) on a given subject (F) in a given kind of literature
3. To assist in the choice of a book (G) as to its edition (bibliographically) (H) as to its character (literary or topical).

With the proviso that (A) (B) and (C) cannot stand independently of each other – a book could not be identified with certainty if only the author, or only the title, or only the subject were known – these objectives have continued to serve as guiding principles in the creation of catalogues, whatever the format in which the catalogue is made available. They were compiled in the era of the printed book catalogue, but are equally applicable to the catalogue on card, fiche, or online. Any librarian working to provide access to a collection could be advised to take these objectives as the starting point in setting qualitative service targets.

Cutter did not stop at setting objectives for the catalogue. He gave the means to the ends as well:

1. Author-entry with the necessary references (for A and D)
2. Title-entry or title-reference (for B)
3. Subject-entry, cross-references and classed subject table (for C and E)
4. Form-entry and language entry (for F)
5. Giving edition and imprint, with notes when necessary (for G)
6. Notes (for H)[3].

Again, the means have stood the test of time in terms of underpinning the theory of information organization. Cutter set his rules in the context of a dictionary catalogue, that is, a catalogue in which the vocabulary-controlled access points for names, titles and subjects are presented in a single alphabetical sequence. This was the predominant form of catalogue in North America. In the United Kingdom, on the other hand, the classified catalogue held sway. The principal structuring element in this catalogue was the classification number. The classified catalogue was able to replicate the order of the items on the shelves, with the bonus of being able to place a record, as item surrogate, at more than one subject location in the catalogue. Shelf location depends on a single classification number representing the principal subject of the item content, but the classified catalogue can place a record for the item at all the additional subject classificatory locations appropriate to the item. Subject access was enhanced, within the framework of the theoretical division of knowledge the classification scheme provided. The dictionary catalogue, which utilized a subject headings scheme to provide its subject access points, was also able to enhance subject access by allocating more than one subject heading to an item, but the alphabetical interfiling of names, titles and subject headings meant that the dictionary catalogue lacked both the overall theoretical framework of the classified catalogue and its ability to display subject relationships.

The specificity of a classification number is often governed not by the actual subject of the work but by the volume of material in the collection on that general subject. The greater the quantity, the more specific the classification number must be to ensure adequate levels of subject clumping. It is at this point that the cataloguer needs to bear in mind that the purpose of vocabulary control, whether it be for name, subject or title, is to provide a point at which records relating to a unique subject, name or title may be found. That uniqueness is defined in terms of the other access points with which it finds itself. The classification number or subject heading needs to be general enough to collocate all the topical works in the collection, but specific enough to distinguish what is being collocated. The name heading needs to be general enough to collocate all the works in the collection relating to the bibliographic identity it represents, but specific enough to distinguish that bibliographic identity from another bibliographic identity represented in the collection with an otherwise identical name. When we consider this concept of specificity, we see that the question of subject indexing at the analytical level introduces far more problems for controlled subject access than it does for name access. A name is a name is a name, whether the named individual is writing a film script, drawing a picture, singing a song, or typing an electronic document. Subject indexing beyond the whole-item level would mean a proportionately greater increase in subject headings than in name headings. In almost all areas but the humanities, subject is the primary means by which collections are arranged and utilized.

We have looked at the way in which the catalogue has developed to become much more than a finding list. By employing internal vocabulary control and by interaction with a classified collection, it works to produce a system of organized access. We have also started to see how this system of organized access cannot and does not stand in isolation from other access tools and processes. We now need to look more closely at the issue of remote access, whether this means access by the library to collections and resources other than its own, or access to the library's resources by users remote from the library site.

Remote access is by no means a new concept for librarians. Apart from the Net surfers, the most frequent checkers of catalogues on the Internet may be librarians looking for a source of material requested by users. The growing ability to share electronic resources – or, more candidly, for the individual library to access and download information provided 'for free' wherever there is a call for it – has prompted debate over the question of 'access versus ownership'. Libraries do not own these electronic materials, but they have access to them when they need them. We might consider that this is the public library system writ large, a system where no single individual owns the resources found in the local library, but every single individual has access to those resources on demand. The difference is, of course, that the resources of a public library are not free, they are provided collectively by the community through taxation. The collection is collectively owned. The material available electronically is provided at the discretion of the institution or individual making the material available.

There have been some interesting studies comparing the behaviour of those people who search a catalogue from outside the

----

library itself, and those using the online catalogue as part of their library visit. Remote users appear to be more sophisticated – if only because they have figured out *how* to access the catalogue remotely. They are also 30% more likely to search the catalogue by name or by title – there are only half as many remote subject searches as take place in the library itself.[4] This is an interesting finding, which supports the theory that remote searching is generally specific-item searching. Many of these searches will be made by librarians looking for sources of interlibrary loans, others by users looking for a source for a single known item. The remote user is seriously disadvantaged in comparison with the searcher on site, whatever type of search is being carried out, because the remote searcher has access only to those catalogues and databases which are computer-readable and, by extension, is made aware only of material for which computer-readable records exit. Access tools such as book indexes, card catalogues and indexes, and fiche products are all unavailable for deeper and wider access to a collection.

Off-the-peg access

What happens when a member of the library's user community asks for an item that the library does not possess? The library will supply the item from a remote source, whether that remote source is another library or a computer which stores the required item in electronic form. The latter is quicker, but it can be more expensive in both cost of download (in monetary and time terms) and cost of provision of hard copy. Interlibrary loan enhances access in the sense of providing materials not immediately physically available to the searcher in the library; it supplements the service provided on site.

The advent of the new technologies has meant that libraries now do much more to make available to their users tools which identify a broader range of information and material than is recorded in the catalogue. They do not as yet provide access to large quantities of data in electronic form, and indeed there are not vast quantities of full text files available to access. Libraries are hesitant to substitute access for ownership, precisely because the bargain is not that of the interlibrary loan system. In many cases, to prefer access to ownership is to tie the library to the commercial organization making the data available – and, as we have seen, buying the right to access a database is not the same as buying information in the form of a discrete item such as a book. The focus shifts from the choice to purchase on the part of the buyer to the choice as to what to provide on the part of the supplier – a broadcast service medium rather than a commodity-based medium. A second consequence for libraries choosing access over ownership is that, in terms of staff resources, they will require more people in reader services and fewer in technical services. Again, this has the consequence of lessening the perceived value of cataloguing, making it an increasingly invisible service to librarians as well as to users.

In an article considering the access-versus-ownership question, Irene Hoadley makes the following observation: 'Think about businesses that tried to stock everything attempting to meet the needs of all comers. Most have gone the way of the dinosaur.'[5] The parallel is preposterous. No library has ever attempted to 'stock everything', and any that was so abundantly blessed with funding as to attempt to do so would undoubtedly perish. Libraries are not businesses, supplying the demands of individual library customers. They are supplying the needs of their user communities, and, vitally, anticipating their future needs. They have to have the professional skills and abilities to be able to forecast which kinds of needs are going to be either so large a volume of their 'business' that they must provide them direct on site, or so important qualitatively for the 'business' of the community that they must provide access to them on site. The needs of the community are paramount.

'Access versus ownership' is an old concept under a new guise. Libraries have cooperated between themselves for years, sharing their resources in order to focus their acquisitions spending. Interlibrary lending is a genuine form of cooperation – from each according to means to each according to need. Remote access to documents involves most libraries in taking and few in giving, with the ultimate creation of a dependency culture from which few libraries will be able to escape. If economic pressures and the imposition of the market ethos promote the concept of access over ownership, then the evaluation measures used to compile a statistical profile of the value of the library must not function on simple counting of stock, but on the remote access services provided by the library as well. It is important that librarians do not get caught in the circular argument that reads 'less money – less stock – less important – less money'.

The librarian as customer

One group of users of databases of bibliographic records which does not receive much attention, but whose requirements have probably had an inordinate and disproportionate influence on access, are librarians themselves. As acquisitions budgets are cut, librarians have sought means of supplying requested items other than purchase. Running in parallel, librarians have sought out other sources of catalogue records to import into their catalogues as the resources to provide original cataloguing are stretched ever more thinly. Both these trends have emphasized the retrieval of records relating to known, specific items. As we have seen, this type of search is at variance with the requirements of researchers, who are generally looking, not for items of which they are already aware, but for unknown items associated with or of relevance to the topic they are researching. In their constant search for answers to record provision and item provision the professional staff who are building the catalogues and collections can easily lose sight of the integrated and interdependent nature of the catalogue, the collection and the classification scheme, and their unique ability to answer such complex questions.

The bibliographic utilities such as OCLC and the Research Libraries Information Network (RLIN) have become major players in the provision of bibliographic records, and by extension in the access available to many collections. At the whole item level, the records in the databases of these utilities follow international standards such as the International Standard Bibliographic Description (ISBD) and MARC (MAchine Readable Cataloguing – a communications format which standardizes the structure, content and coding of computer-readable bibliographic records). It is in the interests of the bibliographic utilities to supply records in this standard form if they are to be assured entry to the largest possible market for catalogue records. As far as access to automated databases of analytical-level material is concerned, however, the profit motive has probably militated against standardization. As most libraries provide only partial access to their collections at this analytical level, they are usually in the position of taking what is available. Amongst the thousands of differing databases which cover the material, the means of searching and retrieving data are continually changing – as indeed are the products themselves as businesses start up, merge or fold. Database suppliers will often build in a nonstandard, individual approach to avoid copyright infringements and suits by competitors, as well as committing purchasers to stay loyal to the product.

The US Department of Education has recently awarded a $62,000 grant to support an OCLC project 'Building a Catalog of Internet Resources'.[6] This initiates a nationwide coordinated effort amongst both libraries and institutions of higher education to create and evaluate a searchable database of bibliographic records for material accessible over the Internet. The records will be in MARC format and will include electronic location and access information. This approach is the right way to handle provision of records for electronic information accessible remotely rather than held in local library databases, and extends the concept of the bibliographic utility. These remotely accessible resources should be catalogued once, and the records should form, not a part of the catalogue of the library accessing the remote database, but a separate catalogue of the resources on the remote host. This is in line with the model of nested and interdependent levels of access discussed earlier.

Through a combination of cuts in funding and the drive to impose and respond to market forces in providing access to the means of acquiring knowledge, activities which enhance, enrich and give added value to the catalogue are progressively being ignored, removed or 'automated'. Increasingly, the library may no longer be willing or able to invest in the provision of information regarding other relevant materials in its collection, placing the onus on the individual to discover this information each time it is required. These cuts in the enhanced access that the professional techniques of librarianship can provide are often disguised under public sound bites and technological hype suggesting that access to the collection is being improved; but we should not be fooled. Simplistic keyword searching of a database is better than nothing, but it in no way replicates the much richer and deeper access to the contents of a collection that the intellectual application of professional library skills can provide. In the attempt to show that our libraries are giving value for money by providing speedy and effective access to specific items, we are in the long term dramatically lessening the full market value of our organized systems and at the same time failing to exploit the full potential of our collections. We have to invest for the future.

References

1 Tyckoson, David, 'The 98% solution', *Technicalities*, **9** (2), February 1989.
2 *Life: the Observer magazine*, 7 May 1995, 5.
3 Cutter, Charles Ammi, *Rules for a dictionary catalog*, 4th edn, rewritten, Washington, 1904.
4 Sloan, Bernard G., 'Remote access: design implications for online catalogues', in *Enhancing access to information*, New York, The Haworth Press, 1991.
5 Hoadley, Irene B., 'Access vs. ownership', *Library acquisitions*, **17** (2), 1993, 191.
6 *OCLC newsletter*, September/October 1994, 5.

CHAPTER 4
STANDARDS FOR SHARING

The why and the wherefore

Every library is in business to enable the sharing of the content of its collection of recorded knowledge and information. The collection is naturally provided primarily for the profit of the funding user community; but to their mutual benefit libraries increasingly share their collections with others, providing physically or electronically on site only those materials judged of primary utility to the user community. Standards form the basis of that sharing.

Bibliographic standards can be defined as those standards which, when applied to a collection of recorded knowledge, organize and facilitate access to the knowledge records and their intellectual content. They are therefore of value not just in libraries, but in information units, in single or multimedia collections and in bookshops or stores selling all kinds of media. Bibliographic standards are also of value in creating various listings of collections, although not all bibliographic standards are necessary for all types of listing. Fundamentally, bibliographic standards are an absolute requirement when bibliographic information is used to fulfil more than a single function.

We can divide bibliographic standards into those standards which are needed for the effective organization of and access to the collection and its content – such as cataloguing rules, classification schemes, lists of subject headings and other vocabulary-controlled lists of names and titles, and those standards which can be defined as 'trade' standards – standards which facilitate the control and exchange of data about books and other media as physical entities. Examples of 'trade' standards are the International Standard Book Number (ISBN) and the International Standard Serial Number (ISSN). Playing another part in the bibliographic information sys-

tem are standards which enable the communication of bibliographic data, such as MARC and Electronic Data Interchange
(EDI).

Bibliographic standards present a varied pattern of origin and
development. Some have developed by accident, others by design,
and most by a combination of the two. In an article in the *Library
Association record,* Ross Bourne has defined three categories of standard: the official, the quasi-official, and the *de facto.*[1] Official standards see the light of day through the design of national or
international standards institutions such as the British Standards
Institution (BSI) or the International Standards Institution (ISO).
None of the principal Anglo-American bibliographic standards fall
into this category. The quasi-official standards are those created and
maintained through international or national professional or trade
bodies like the International Federation of Library Associations
(IFLA) or Book Industry Communication (BIC). Finally the *de facto*
standards such as the Library of Congress Subject Headings
(LCSH) or the Anglo-American Cataloguing Rules (AACR) are
created and controlled by independent institutions or consortia, but
have gained a wide degree of authority and acceptance through the
backing of major players in the bibliographic market-place.

We can see the importance that endorsement by major players
has in establishing a standard by looking at the example of the CD-
audio market. The so-called 'Red Book standard' was rapidly
adopted worldwide, with the result that it took only one year to
achieve sales of one million CD-audio players – as compared to five
years to sell one million video players, where a single standard format took a much longer time to evolve. A standard does not
become a standard because it has the approval of a standards institution like ISO. It becomes a standard when it is accepted by product manufacturers, and above all when it is accepted by a major
corporation such as IBM or Microsoft or Sony. In the library field,
such 'major corporations' are the bibliographic utilities – national
libraries and other institutions which support a developed bibliographic service.

Standards are of most benefit when they are both created and
endorsed at the highest level. The major cataloguing standards in

use in the United Kingdom are a mixture of internationally created and endorsed standards and of standards owned by specific institutions but whose content is maintained by independent committees, or otherwise supported by external input to the development of the standard. The Anglo-American Cataloguing Rules (AACR) was created and is endorsed by the American Library Association, the British Library, the Canadian Library Association, The Library Association, the Library of Congress and the National Library of Canada. The Dewey Decimal Classification is owned by OCLC but its content is maintained by an editorial committee with British representation. Library of Congress Subject Headings (LCSH) is owned and controlled by the Library of Congress, but external individuals and institutions are increasingly able to contribute to the standard as influential consumers.

The preparation and agreement of standards is a time-consuming and resource-intensive business, but that is not the end of the matter – standards have to actually be applied to produce benefits. A standard may be the most perfect piece of consistency and logic ever crafted by the hand and brain of humankind, but if it is not used it essentially has value only as a museum exhibit. We have the evidence of classification schemes such as the Colon Classification, created by Ranganathan and generally held amongst experts to be technically superior, which, however, remains largely unused. The Preserved Context Indexing System (PRECIS) similarly languishes as no more than an academic curiosity. The failure to adopt standards is firmly lodged in the disturbance to established systems of organization and access which can be brought about by change, particularly when the established systems in question are those of major players. This should not be ascribed to mere head in the sand resistance on the part of cataloguers, or refusal to invest resources on the part of administrators. There is truth in the adage 'if it ain't broke, don't fix it'; present systems, though by no means perfect, are by no means imperfect either and have the merit of a proven track record. We have seen that a library using a classification scheme and a vocabulary-controlled catalogue created in the context of established international cataloguing rules and bibliographic tools can provide a quality of access unrivalled by any mere computer database.

Consistency and uniformity deliver results

Within each separate library catalogue, index, bibliography or other listing, standards have a dual role: they provide internal consistency and they facilitate the systematic access which is at the heart of effective library service. If the listing does not have internal consistency, the user is not only confused but, more importantly, is liable to lose access to useful material. We have seen that when standards change, for example when changes are made to cataloguing codes or new codes are adopted, serious problems can be created for the library in providing comprehensive access to its collection content. Such changes also militate against uniform access throughout a catalogue. Libraries and bibliographic utilities rarely recatalogue when standards change; they rarely even consider recataloguing. We should bear this in mind when changes to standards are being contemplated – not in order to exclude their further development, particularly when this takes place within the context of existing principles, but to ensure that such development does not undermine the systematic basis of the catalogue and means of access to the collection. When the principles underlying standards change, libraries and bibliographic utilities always need to evaluate the ways in which they can bring their existing catalogues and databases into line with the new principles if they are to avoid the pitfalls of split catalogues.

Standards are of particular relevance and importance in retrospective catalogue conversion. If the conversion of a catalogue from manual to automated form is to be of benefit to more than just the library carrying out the conversion, the converted records should conform wherever possible to international standards.[2] This is particularly important when the records are for older or specialized material for which no computer-readable record currently exists. The standards should control both the data content of the bibliographic record and the form it takes, and the data format in which the computer-readable record is held.

Ever since the International Conference on Cataloguing Principles held in Paris in 1961, which led to the International Meeting of Cataloguing Experts in Copenhagen in 1969 and eventually spawned the series of International Standard Bibliographic Descriptions compiled under the aegis of IFLA, most international cataloguing codes have taken an identical approach to producing a standard description of knowledge carriers (the Anglo-American Cataloguing Rules for description closely follow those of the ISBD). Rules for the form and content of vocabulary controlled access points, however, can vary widely between codes. In the sphere of personal name headings, there are differing ways of presenting and structuring headings for royalty and nobility, as well as those names which may include epithets and titles. Corporate names, apart from the continuing debate over which names can conceptually be included in that category and the question of the legitimacy of subordinate entry, usually present problems related to language. For example, should the name be given in the language of the cataloguing agency and of the principal user community, or in the language of the body itself?

A catalogue, index, or other listing must be internally consistent if systematic access is to be maintained. Nowadays catalogues not only have to be internally consistent, however, they also need to achieve consistency one with another. This is increasingly important as more and more records are shared. Record sharing is a result of standardization and is also a catalyst for further standardization. This can be clearly seen in the current drive for common authority files of vocabulary-controlled access points and in the development of common sets of application policies and 'core' bibliographic data which can be used effectively in the maximum number of catalogues and listings with the minimum amount of local editorial intervention.

A good example of the kind of difficulties encountered when searching across databases which have not been created to a common standard can be found by Internet users who visit different file transfer protocol (FTP) sites. These sites contain computer databases of files that can be accessed remotely from other computers, and the files downloaded to the local computer. *CompuServe magazine* recently gave novice users of FTP the following advice:

> ... FTP holdings are organized solely according to the wishes of the person who established the archive. Finding things can be tricky, and knowing what the files you're browsing through actually contain can be difficult, since site directories list only file names and byte sizes. But many sites post an index, which you can find in the root directory ... These ... will vary from [FTP] site to site; some are huge, containing brief descriptions of thousands of files ... Others are incomplete and infrequently updated, and some sites, unfortunately, have no index files at all.[3]

Such warnings return regular library users to a Jurassic MARC era when catalogues and listings were produced according to the personal rulings of local librarians. It is also germane to note that these computer databases of files are classed as archives, and electronic archives, like paper archives, have been singularly resistant to adopting common standards – particularly those espoused by libraries.

Communicating to share

MARC is the most widely used standard for the storage and communication of bibliographic data within the world's libraries. Pointing up its status as the pre-eminent *de facto* communications standard, the Book Trade Electronic Data Interchange Standards (BEDIS) Committee, in a report published in 1988, recommended the use of MARC in all parts of the book trade using bibliographic data. However, MARC is not a single standard and there are a whole family of separate MARC formats in use.

The original MARC format was established by the Library of Congress (LC), and BNBMARC, developed in the United Kingdom, was the first to diverge from it. Despite the number of formats in existence, all can be said to be modelled on one of three formats: USMARC, UKMARC, or UNIMARC. Each of these three formats developed to meet slightly differing bibliographic requirements. The plethora of MARC formats require conversion programs to move the bibliographic data from format to format when machine-readable records are exchanged by libraries. These conversion programs necessarily need money and resources to maintain, and are increasingly seen as a barrier to the efficient communication of bibliographic records internationally. UNIMARC, which was originally intended to function as an 'Esperanto' format into which all the national formats would be convertible, has signally failed to deliver. This is not surprising given the dominance of the United States and USMARC in the bibliographic marketplace.

MARC first appeared in the mid 1960s, when LC decided to automate both its cataloguing and its catalogue search and retrieval functions. It was immediately recognized that not only would automation provide benefits to the Library of Congress, but machine-readable catalogue records would obviously be a bonus to the increasing number of other libraries which already possessed or were developing their own automated systems. It was agreed that the new machine-readable records prepared by LC would include all the data available on the printed catalogue cards distributed by the Library of Congress, and that the best means of ensuring standardization on the record format was to allow it to be designed at the Library of Congress. This early decision effectively cut off the growth of local formats within the United States and allowed LC to maintain its dominant position in catalogue record supply in the US.

LC established a MARC pilot project with four tasks:

1 To set a standard for the communication of machine-readable bibliographic data between libraries;
2 To structure the data in a format which could be modified and adapted within any given library;
3 To include in the record the data elements used by most libraries in their cataloguing; and,
4 To design a format usable by a variety of computers.

In the United Kingdom, MARC's first appearance was in the supply of British National Bibliography (BNB) records to the Library of Congress, followed by a study which looked at the use of machine-readable data in the production of the BNB itself. BNB staff cooperated with LC in developing what became known in the United States as MARC II, BNB's version of which was published in March 1969. Although BNBMARC and LCMARC were both machine formats with identical systems of field tagging and a very high level of identical data content in those fields, the formats did differ substantially in their approach to bibliographic issues. Not only were they intended to fulfil differing primary purposes – in the case of LCMARC to produce catalogue cards, and for BNBMARC to produce the printed BNB – but also the institutions did not share a common cataloguing standard. The first edition of the Anglo-American Cataloguing Rules in use at the time had British and North American texts which differed substantially in some areas.

Put briefly, LCMARC automated the cataloguing produced by LC to its specific and highly developed application policy requirements, whilst BNBMARC reflected BNB practice which was not tied to the demands of one particular library catalogue and was thus able to employ the cataloguing standard more or less as it stood. Differences generated by these requirements that have continued into the present UKMARC and USMARC formats include the use of punctuation between fields and subfields in USMARC, differing ways of treating series and uniform titles, and the use of reference fields in UKMARC – there for the purpose of providing appropriate references in the individual issues and cumulations of the British National Bibliography.

MARC was derived from and conditioned by the requirements of the card catalogue. In an ideal world, the MARC format would already have been restructured to meet the possibilities of cataloguing using automated systems as we now understand them. The fields need to be regrouped, and the purpose of the fixed length fields need to be reconsidered. Libraries are crying out for a multi-dimensional record that would allow the user to drill down in the catalogue through the bibliographic sequence of series, monograph and analytic, and similarly allow catalogue building through the creation of records at any one of these levels. Unfortunately, such development seems unlikely given both the lack of a single MARC format and the intensely democratic and consultative systems in place for maintenance of the MARC formats in the US and in the UK. The emergence of technical standards such as standard generalized markup language (SGML), which may have the potential to function as the standard for a fully integrated information system, will be considered in the final chapter.

Automated systems need standards, too

Libraries have come a long way down the road of internationally accepted and used standards for recording those bibliographic elements relating to descriptive, item-specific data such as title, publisher and physical format, and also for organizational and integrative data elements such as subject headings, classification numbers and standardized forms of names and works. The means by which all of these bibliographic data elements are held and communicated has also been standardized, largely through the development of the family of MARC formats. However, the means by which the bibliographic data elements are held and accessed presents a much less happy picture. If they are to function effectively, automated systems demand adherence to standards. Automated systems are much less forgiving than human systems – if a single letter is miskeyed by the searcher or by the person inputting the data, a record may be unfindable in a search employing the miskeyed term.

Unlike the bibliographic data created by individual libraries, the automated systems of individual libraries may not communicate with each other. Vendors of automated bibliographic systems often find themselves in the position of having to produce multiple interfaces to talk to the systems of other vendors. We all know the frustrations of sharing even a simple thing like a document, when that document has been produced on word-processing software from one commercial organization and we need to read it on software from another. We tend to accept such things as an irritating but unavoidable fact of life, whilst continuing to laud the wonders of the word-processor. Libraries have achieved something of incredible value in working together to create conditions that allow a bibliographic record to be created in one library and put in the catalogue of another, whilst not losing in the process any of the quality of access provided by the record in its original environment.

Within automated bibliographic systems there is still great scope for increased standardization with regard to those user interfaces such as commands, syntax and choice of data elements to be indexed, all of which can vary widely within different systems. Libraries already have instantaneous access to a wide variety of electronic resources, as we have seen in earlier chapters. However, the continuing proliferation of search languages and differing practices regarding which terms and data are to be indexed put a considerable burden on the user and a considerable training burden on the library if its means of access are to be used effectively.

Searching hundreds of databases with the same search software is one of the advantages of online access over standalone CD-ROM or local databases. The ability to carry out multifile searching, using services such as that provided by DIALOG's One Search, substantially reduces advance preparation time on the part of the searcher and online time for the institution financing the search. However, the reality of such multifile searches is that the databases searched are still separate entities, with many different structures. Across databases, fields may have different names for the same content, or the same name but differing data content. Standardizing the name of a field is relatively easy, but standardizing values within the field is much less so – a situation with which cataloguers wishing to exchange catalogue records are all too conversant. There is no difficulty in devising and establishing a catalogue record format which designates a field to contain a name heading, but a great deal of difficulty in ensuring that the form of name as it appears in that field will be identical amongst libraries using the format, even when they are using the same cataloguing standards. To ensure consistency of data content, standard tools in the shape of authority files have to be established and used.

The professional skills a library invests in creating catalogues providing high-quality access to the recorded knowledge they describe and control must be used effectively by the automated system accommodating the catalogue. This is a field in which cataloguers, who understand the purpose and operation of the access systems they create, must communicate effectively with systems developers and one in which the expertise of cataloguers must be used effectively by systems developers.

The automated catalogue is not just any conventional database of records which the computer software is required to manipulate and structure; it already contains elements that have been designed and applied to enable the bibliographical and intellectual integration of the records. The access and retrieval software must make best use of this data. Technology on its own is of next to no value: technology is there as an enabling mechanism, facilitating the storage, manipulation, communication and provision of access to data. No technology, however state-of-the-art, can make up for missing, inadequate, or incorrectly structured cataloguing data.

Applying the principles

In an interesting study, Ling Hwey Jeng has looked at the suitability of the Anglo-American Cataloguing Rules to form part of the knowledge base of an expert system. If they prove capable of development, expert systems will automate some of the decision-making processes in cataloguing. Jeng draws the conclusion that, because of the large number of rules for transcription and their level of detail for specific conditions and actions, AACR2 '. . . as a standard, is designed to be a device to ensure the consistency of presentation of bibliographic data in cataloguing records to the minute details. It is intended to be a quality control device for inputting bibliographic data into a library catalog'.[4] Even more interestingly, this leads to the suggestion that the high level of detail in the bibliographic conditions covered in the rules leaves little room for either individual cataloguer judgment or for local practices. The standard is therefore more concerned with promoting shared cataloguing amongst professional librarians than the needs of local users of that cataloguing. This is an insightful conclusion and one that is not entirely inaccurate, but it does not pay due attention to the fact that the needs of all users are better met by the consistency that use of an international standard brings, and that arguments for local needs are often founded on uncritical acceptance of past practice rather than a genuine assessment of current possibilities.

Ling Hwey Jeng believes that although the arrangement of the rules in AACR2 is incompatible with the principles of database design, this does not mean that they are inappropriate as guidelines for constructing a library catalogue. Taken together with other standards, such as the ISBD for the inclusion and ordering of bibliographic data and the MARC format for converting bibliographic data from printed format to machine-readable format, they can fulfil this purpose. However, to use the standard to do more than this would '. . . possibly require the designers and revisers of the AACR2 to reduce the number of rules of very limited applicability level and to enhance the rule contents for application domains other than transcription'.[5]

The vexed question of the frequency of use of cataloguing rules has been addressed in a project described by Josef Abrera and Debora Shaw. The practice collection of 716 books in the Indiana University School of Library and Information Science was analysed to establish which of the rules in the second edition of the Anglo-American Cataloguing Rules were used in the production of a catalogue record consisting of bibliographic description and headings. Of the books in the collection, 98% were English-language monographs and almost 60% were works of single authorship; a bare 2% were considered of 'complex' authorship. This would not be unusual in a general library collection, although one is prompted to wonder at the extent of 'practice' the students cataloguing this particular collection were being given.

The results of the project showed that 'relatively few rules account for most of the uses'. Of the rules in Chapter 21 dealing with choice of main entry (the access point to be used in single citation listings) 45 of the 143 rules were used. Chapter 22, dealing with form of personal name, achieved a usage rate of 28.3%, and Chapter 24, dealing with corporate names, 31.8%. The rate fell to 22.6% of the rules in Chapter 25, covering uniform titles (vocabulary-controlled headings for intellectual works). The project was able to define a core set of 25 rules which users needed to know in order to be able to understand the nature of the bibliographic record.

The authors of the article draw an interesting conclusion:

In a way, this empirical study upholds Osborn's call in the early 1940s for a practical rather than a legalistic approach to the 'crisis in cataloguing'. Faced with overwhelming complexity in rules and interpretations, Osborn suggested that 'rules for cataloguing would be relatively few and simple'. We now have evidence that most books can be catalogued with a set of pragmatically derived core rules.[6]

This kind of research is useful, but we have to be careful to interpret the results in the right way. We are in danger of falling into the trap of once again establishing 'usage' as the sole measure of value. It is one measure, but to concentrate on usage exclusively is to give only a part of the picture. It is incorrect to draw the inference that rules – like journals – which are not used frequently are of no value, or indeed, necessarily of less value. We could say that their availability to answer a less frequently asked question is a measure of their higher value. This same point regarding 'usage' is frequently made in the analysis of resource-intensive authority control work, with proponents of the simplification of cataloguing school suggesting that we should invest resources in establishing a vocabulary-controlled form only for a name which occurs more than once in the catalogue. Of course, we do not know which names are going to occur again when they first come to the attention of the cataloguer; but, much more importantly, the catalogue is greater than the sum of its individual records. You cannot provide a partial system of bibliographic control to a catalogue and to a collection if they are to attain their optimum level of performance.

Library of Congress Subject Headings (LCSH) are the single most important example of a *de facto* standard that is not based on any codified set of principles. There have been a number of calls for such codification over the years, and these have become louder as cooperative cataloguing schemes have developed, demanding readily understandable and applicable shared standards. During the 1980s there was a move away from the discussion of language, currency and bias in terminology, which had until then dominated criticism of the LC subject headings, to questions of relationship, reference and hierarchy, marking an interest in the systematic structure of the headings when working together in an access system such as a catalogue. At present, although the Library of Congress has shown itself increasingly open to outside participation in the modification and improvement of LCSH, there is no plan of action for producing a set of principles for the creation of the headings which could act as the foundation for a genuine subject access system. In some ways, the principles are evolving from the application policies, in a sort of back-to-the-future approach to establishing a subject code. Although illogical and inconsistent, this approach has the merit of pragmatism and minimal disruption to established authority files of subject headings.

Subject headings systems such as LCSH were devised for and developed in the context of the card catalogue. The relational, binding structure that guides the searcher from term to term and which performs a critical role in the card catalogue can be used much more flexibly in the online catalogue, making the intellectual resources invested in the creation and maintenance of this systematic linking far more cost-effective. The online catalogue not only releases the search potential of every term in the heading; it also allows the reference structure to be hidden from the user. The step-by-step search process in the card catalogue, whereby the searcher must manually move from uncontrolled to controlled form of term, can be carried out by the computer on the basis of the embedded links created by the cataloguer. Key in an uncontrolled term, and you are automatically provided with records bearing the controlled terms – as long as the cataloguer has put in the links for the machine to follow.

William E. Studwell, who has been the major protagonist for a subject code based on the standardization of LC subject headings, makes some eloquent and effective points in stating that a subject code is

> ... simply the standardization of subject headings and their application, plus documentation of the standards ... Let us hope that the subject code is not dead, for if it is, standardization of LC subject headings is also dead. In an increasingly complex age, lack of standardization of

any technical system or process tends to lead to the demise of the system or process.[7]

The dominance of the Library of Congress in the bibliographic market may, however, make the death scene one of the longest in history.

A development which would have a great deal of theoretical merit is the extension of AACR to cover subject headings. Part II of AACR, which deals with access points, already strays into this area in Chapter 23, which contains rules for establishing controlled forms of geographic names. Geographical locations are unlikely ever to feature as responsible for intellectual content of a work; they are, however, exceedingly common as an aspect of subject access. The Dewey Decimal Classification has already brought the appearance of geographic names in the classification into line with AACR, and the British Library COMPASS (Computer Assisted Subject Searching) subject system similarly uses AACR principles in establishing the vocabulary-controlled form of name of geographic features. It seems unlikely though that the Library of Congress would be willing to lose its market dominance in the field of subject headings by actively driving or supporting such a development of AACR. It would be fascinating to discover whether it would be possible to weave principles that would support LCSH into the existing AACR framework.

To be successful, a subject search has to entail as close to complete as possible coordination between the terms used to express the subject by the user and those provided by the system. Failure to achieve this match will result in less than comprehensive retrieval of relevant material from the collection. The cause may lie in deficiencies in one of three areas. Firstly, the subject analysis may be faulty because either the author is unable to clearly express the subject of his or her work, or the cataloguer is lacking the expertise to understand and analyse the subject. Secondly, the subject system may not be capable of allowing the expression of the subject in a way which will occur to the user. Both classification schemes and subject indexing schemes face the continual problem of having to reflect current conceptual approaches to the organization of know-

ledge, while maintaining stability in the way in which subject access
is provided within a collection and its catalogue. Finally, the technological system used to store the subject terms and headings and
to process the search may be deficient.

The key stage in this process of matching the approaches of
searcher and catalogue is the subject analysis of the work by the cataloguer. The process is by its very nature fuzzy and indeterminate,
but this also militates against its subordination to machine processing. 'After everything else in bibliographic control has been programmed into a computer, this area will remain the domain of
human judgement.'[8] There is continuing research into ways of shifting the emphasis from this initial subject analysis stage towards the
use of user interfaces and expert systems in moving the searcher
through the search process. To date, all research shows that human
intervention is necessary to provide an acceptable level of quality
retrieval from a collection.

The options for application

Unfortunately the most rigorous application of standards does not
always offer an absolute guarantee of consistency. One difficulty
encountered by all standards, whether bibliographic or technical, is
that of options. Options enable choice and allow a certain degree of
flexibility at the local level. The Anglo-American Cataloguing
Rules, despite the continuing work of alignment of practice and
reduction of options carried out for its second edition, still allow a
choice of rule in a number of important situations. When libraries
choose to apply different options, the catalogue records they produce will work less effectively in each other's catalogues.

The answer to this problem of choice in the application of standards is to continue to work to reduce the number of options, whenever this can be done without substantial detriment to the
functional ability of the record to facilitate access to a specific local
collection. Where options are considered necessary to maintain this
functionality, we should extend as widely as possible the development of common application policies for the standard, so that those
libraries contributing records to a shared database will know which
options are to be used, and those libraries taking records from a

shared database will know which parts of the records they take may need amendment in the context of the receiving library catalogue.

Those AACR2 'options' which relate to language are a good example of necessary options. The catalogue of a library serving a Welsh-speaking community, for example, will approach optimum effectiveness only if the catalogue records use the Welsh language in all data elements other than those which are purely transcriptive. However, what may be a required policy in the local environment can cause real difficulties when that library is using and contributing to shared bibliographic tools such as authority files, or using and contributing to shared databases of catalogue records. The major cooperative programmes, whether at the regional, national, or international level, have all been based on single-language tools and databases. Common tools for multiple-language cooperative communities are the next step forward, but this should not lead us to undervalue or undermine the important cooperative developments in the application of standards that have taken place over the last 20 to 30 years.

The most well known and widely used standard set of application policies is the Library of Congress Rule Interpretations (LCRI), which developed on the basis of the application policies needed within a specific institution. It is easier (although by no means easy) to rigorously control the application of standards within a single library environment. The growth of copy cataloguing and the growth of retrospective catalogue conversions, however, within even the largest and most important of single library environments, have radically increased the import and export of records that do not necessarily conform to the same application policies. Such is the volume of LCRI that libraries wishing to share records are often not prepared to commit themselves to cooperative programmes which demand that the LCRI be followed comprehensively. The Library of Congress is now looking closely at the LCRI to define those that are essential to maintain the quality of the catalogue as a system of structured access to a collection.

Standards in stone?

The argument is sometimes made that standards stifle innovation, and that the further they extend their tentacles and the more pervasive they become, the harder it is to rethink the functions they deliver in the light of developing technology and the differing uses to which bibliographic records may be put. There is an element of surface appeal in this argument, but it is based on the assumption that technological change somehow invalidates the original purpose for which the standards were developed. It seems less than likely that the fundamental purpose of the library in acquiring, describing, and making available the intellectual content of its collection will ever change. When considering substantive change to basic bibliographic standards, we have first to decide whether they still enable the effective description of and access to recorded knowledge. We also have to take account of the fact that the primary means of access to recorded knowledge often differs according to the nature of the medium in which the knowledge is recorded, the purpose of the collection, or the needs of the user. A collection of newspaper cuttings, for example, will have little need for descriptive standards but a fundamental need for subject indexing standards. A filing cabinet of documents has similar access requirements. A database of electronic documents may well have the same. Fitness for purpose is an appropriate measure of a standard.

In recent years the most significant change to bibliographic standards has been the introduction in 1978 of the second edition of the Anglo-American Cataloguing Rules. Although the line taken at the time by its proponents was to downplay the significance of the changes made between editions, in theoretical terms they were substantial. The reality of the situation on the ground, however, was that when they adopted AACR2 libraries were, by and large, not moving from one uniformly implemented standard to another but from the chaos of catalogues created by layer upon layer of previous practice to a single uniform standard. This was especially true in the United States, where opposition to the introduction of AACR2 was particularly heated because of the scale of change its adoption implied in catalogues that reflected the geological strata of LC practice.

It is interesting to speculate on whether the same depth of antagonism would have existed in the United Kingdom, had it also been in the position of having a national library which had played a long-standing role in providing catalogue records for the libraries of the country. Instead, the role of central catalogue record provider was played by the British National Bibliography, which had not only consistently used current standards but had also played an active part in their development. BNB did not have a catalogue to maintain and so was not faced with the problems of change and the weight of history which hamstrung all large libraries elsewhere. Now that the British National Bibliography is an integral part of the British Library, and now that the BL catalogues are much more closely aligned and integrated with international standards, questioning of change which cannot be justified in cost-effective terms can perhaps be expected to be more significant.

Shared standards, shared application policies and shared bibliographic tools all work to facilitate the production of a bibliographic record of optimum utility. We now need to consider the way in which the market environment may impact on the cooperative task of sharing.

References

1 Bourne, Ross, 'Standards: who needs them?', *Library Association record*, **96** (3), March 1994, 148–9.

2 Süle, Gisela, 'Bibliographic standards for retrospective conversion', *IFLA journal*, **16** (1), 1990, 58–63.

3 'Discovering FTP', *CompuServe magazine*, March 1995, 28.

4 Jeng, Ling Hwey, 'The structure of a knowledge base for cataloging rules', *Information processing and management*, **27** (1), 1991, 108.

5 Jeng, Ling Hwey, 'The structure of a knowledge base for cataloging rules', *Information processing and management*, **27** (1), 1991, 109.

6 Abrera, Josef and Shaw, Debora, 'Frequency of use of cataloguing rules in a practice collection', *Library resources and technical*

services, **36** (2), April 1992, 152.

7   Studwell, William H., 'Who killed the subject code?', *Technical services quarterly*, **12** (1), 1994, 41.

8   Hagler, Ronald, *The bibliographic record and information technology*, 2nd edn, Chicago, ALA, 1991.

CHAPTER 5
MENDING THE MARKET

We live in interesting times. The 'Information Age' competes with the 'New Age' for media coverage, the doings of the electronic travellers on the Infobahn with those of the more land-locked souls avoiding the net of the Criminal Justice Act. Both have an individualist ethos which is at odds with the collectivist, public service ideals of the library movement. The New Age travellers, like their fellow protesters against many of the economic forces of the time and their social outcome, contrast with the lonely, opted-out cybernauts of virtual reality. Standards are held to impose a rigidity and conformity inimical to both groups and yet, as we have seen, the global economy and its major players demand standardization and ruthlessly narrow the options for real choice amongst consumers. We see the impact of this global standardization in all aspects of our daily life, including some of the most formative for any community. Of the 6000 languages thought to exist currently on earth, 95% will probably disappear within the next hundred years. Many believe that language death should be celebrated, not mourned, because it hastens the consolidation of the global village, in which goods can be freely traded and information readily shared.[1]

We have seen that libraries, like any business, need standards if their enterprise is to flourish. The profits which ensue from conformity to and use of standards fall to the library's 'shareholders', its funding community, in more effective access to the contents of their collection and more efficient utilization of resources. Librarians are managing their business efficiently if they trade good-quality records, valued and sought after in the bibliographic market-place, which maximize the profits of their investors and retain the loyalty of their customers. This chapter looks at the way in which standards operate in the bibliographic market-place.

Do our present standards meet the market?

The most fervent advocates of the electronic storage and communication of information hold that it is a concept so mould-breaking in its nature that it entirely invalidates those bibliographic standards concerned with the description of a carrier of recorded knowledge. Without much stronger evidence than this hand-waving assertion, we must at least question whether the 'Information Age' indeed needs new, or even radically changed, bibliographic standards if it is to continue to meet the demands of the market in information control and access. The systematic approach to the organization of information which results from the application of standards, and which has been developed by libraries over the last 150 years, is an asset of great value – far too great to risk its destruction in any lemming-like dash to prove that cataloguers can see the emperor's new clothes of the electronic library.

Cataloguers, despite the fact that they have always been at the leading edge of the practical application of technology within libraries, continue to take a masochistic pleasure in being told how out of touch they are and how irrelevant their systems of bibliographic control. Evidence of this trait is found in a paper by Derek Law, given to the Library Association's Cataloguing & Indexing Group seminar in Retford in 1994. In this piece cataloguers are condemned as 'style fascists', lacking in knowledge of the latest electronic wizardry, and the guardians of out-dated, unnecessary standards which should immediately be consigned to the dustbin of history.[2] Nor is this sort of attack by any means uncommon. The electronic evangelists assert that soon 'everything' will be in electronic form and that AACR and other bibliographic standards developed for a non-electronic world are, therefore, 'irrelevant'. Yet libraries continue to use these bibliographic standards to provide a quality of access to their collections unparalleled by anything in the underdeveloped electronic world.

In an interesting article in the *Wall Street journal*, reprinted in the *Observer*, Umberto Eco considered the question of whether the 'images of the global village will destroy the written page'[3] and the current resurrection of interest in the prophecies of Marshall

McLuhan. Eco rightly argued that in fact computer screens display far more letters than pictures. In some ways technological developments have been regressive, and we are being led, not into a Promised Land, but into a more tightly restrictive linear, text-based world than any we have known in the past. Pictures are not always superior to words. A picture may tells a thousand stories, but when time is of the essence and certainty a necessity, a few well-chosen words may be preferable. The PC screen limits rather than expands the power of words and pictures. When we hold a book, when we consult a print or card catalogue, when we enter a real library, thousands of small signals act on our subconscious to give us a sense of structure and organization. Acting on these signals, we can quickly locate information that is of value, using the embedded systematic framework provided by the author and the librarian and enhanced by the use of standards. Sitting alone in front of the PC screen, we see only what is immediately in front of us. We have no structural context, no spatial context.

Eco, recognizing that computers encourage text, then posed the question of whether they will make books obsolete. He draws the conclusion that computers will, indeed, mark the end of books such as encyclopaedias and other reference tools. The production of this kind of work on CD-ROM not only enables the inclusion of audio and video material, but more importantly it also expands access, in the same way that a computer catalogue can potentially bring together records in an infinity of ways and thereby increase the routes by which the collection content can be approached. This conclusion is fascinating. It points up a fact which has been staring cataloguers in the face for the last 20 years. Computers are very good at manipulating small packets of information such as catalogue records; they are able to make comprehensive machine links, pulling together records related by data held in common. On the other hand any work which requires sustained reading, viewing or listening, together with speculation and reflection on its content, has a need for intellectual and physical organization which is most successfully communicated through a medium other than the computer. A catalogue interacting with a classified collection of items brings together aspects of the two – it consists of small independent

packets of information, but these packets require systematic organization and intellectual relational linking to make the library work
as an integrated whole. It is the process of organizing and linking
that adds value to the catalogue, and it is the use of standards which
turns that organization and linking into a system of bibliographic
access and control.

Books, films, audio tapes, videos, CDs, online databases, will all
continue to exist because each of these media of communication
best fulfils a specific human need within the limitations of a specific
time and place. All will continue to need systematic organization by
the cataloguer to allow high-quality access to their intellectual contents. This high-quality access is the result of the application of our
developed bibliographic standards. The problem is not that our
bibliographic standards do not allow such access, or are not capable of providing effective access to all material and at all analytical
levels of a bibliographic item. The problem lies, as it always has,
with a lack of resources to fully apply the standards, not necessarily
with any failings of the standards themselves.

The attention paid by librarians to the electronic age and the
electronic library is a frivolous distraction from the attention we
should be paying to those economic and social forces which pose a
potentially catastrophic threat to our systems of bibliographic
access and to the standards on which they are built. We cannot but
be aware of the dominance of market-based theory and the individualism on which it is founded. This theory has been dogmati-
cally applied throughout every political, economic and social
strand of our lives. It has hit the public service professions – those
professions which are seeking a social rather than an economic
result from what they do – particularly harshly. The library exists
to serve its user community. It is funded by its community on the
understanding that its services will then be free at the point of use.
The library collection has been organized so as to allow a systematic means of access to both the physical items themselves and the
intellectual content of those physical items. The librarian organizes
information so that it can be used, and in the process of that use
knowledge is acquired – knowledge which benefits the entire community.

Such a collectivist approach is barely comprehensible to the marketeers, who do not, of course, acknowledge the existence of society. They are much happier with the concept of the electronic library, which focuses attention not on the communication of knowledge but on the individual search for information. Information is much more amenable to the theory of the market than knowledge. It can be measured, it can be priced, it is a commodity which can be bought and sold. Librarians are information brokers – without the high pay rates of their colleagues in the City, naturally. Library administrators prefer hard information to soft knowledge, because in their harassed search for economic efficiency it is so much easier to use the satisfaction of specific information needs as a measure of performance and success.

The concept of the electronic library can be said to represent the high-water mark of individualism, and the concentration on known-information, specific-item searching which has been one of the by-products of computer catalogues and computerized record creation. The real objectives of any library are much more complex, much more demanding, and inherently much more beneficial to the development of the community. To focus entirely on specific information searching means the inevitable return of the catalogue to its origins as a pure and simple finding list. We as librarians are increasingly losing our understanding of the collocative function of the catalogue, and how it must interact with the classified collection to enable full access not just to the physical, but to the intellectual contents of the library. Without this understanding, we cannot appreciate our standards and we cannot defend their importance in a resource-hungry environment. Without bibliographic standards libraries will die.

Those standards which are developed and agreed by official standards institutions or by other publicly accountable bodies or consortia are expected to operate democratically, but even in the world of standards the social and economic changes of the last 15 years have left their mark. In 1990 the British Standards Institution (BSI) transferred its information technology-related activities, including those of its documentation committees, to a newly established body named DISC – Delivery Information Solutions to

Customers through International Standards. DISC operates as a division of BSI, but with the important distinction that standards formulation is carried out only by those institutions prepared to pay its separate subscription. It is the suppliers to the market, rather than the consumers, who make the rules. Like everything else, standards are now expected to be commercially self-supporting, in that their sales are expected to finance their future development costs:

> BSI's apparently democratic approach may, after all, be subject to the accident of who can afford or is invited to take part rather than what is best for the library and information community. This is not to denigrate the contribution of any participant to BSI work, but the rules of what are fundamentally those of the market place seem inappropriate to the exercise of our profession.[4]

Such a reaction is entirely understandable, but it is to ignore history and the way in which other *de facto* professional standards are financed. To take the Anglo-American Cataloguing Rules as an example, royalties from sales of the code go into an AACR Fund, managed by the consortium of AACR author bodies, which then finances meetings of the Joint Steering Committee for Revision of AACR and other projects related to AACR. Without sales, the code cannot be developed. This puts those responsible for the content of the rules into a difficult situation. Change will generate sales and finance future sales, but change may not be in the best interest of the institutions supporting and using the code, and it may not even be necessary to enhance information access and control. Standards, whatever their origin, never exist in a moral vacuum. There are many parallels here with the marketing of upgrades to computer software. Constant change is necessary to generate revenue, and the customer must be induced to buy. In the case of bibliographic standards, however, the major standards are not only developed by the major bibliographic institutions but are also used by them to organize large, complex integrated systems of control and access. This acts as a useful rein on change for the sake of change.

A constant theme of this book is the need for librarians to develop ways of presenting what they do to in language that will fit comfortably into the current ethos of the world in which we live. Only in this way can we present a case which will be listened to in the fight for resources, and only with resources can we continue to provide and expand the high-quality access to information which libraries provide and which the market requires. The following definition is taken from an article by Sandra Ward which appeared in *Aslib proceedings*. It effectively supports the position that standards play as important a role in the trading of information as they do in any other:

> Standards aim to promote trade by the removal of barriers caused by differences in national practices; to protect consumer interests through adequate and consistent quality of goods and services; to promote economy in human effort, materials and energy in the production and exchange of goods; to promote the quality of life, safety and health and the protection of the environment; to provide a means of communication between all interested parties; and to encourage co-operation in economic, intellectual, technological and scientific endeavours.[5]

Although couched in the language of the market, with its talk of promoting trade and protecting consumer interests, this definition expresses exactly the benefit of standards in the work of libraries and cataloguing. I now want to analyse those benefits in more detail.

Standards promote trade and increase the market size

First of all, let us examine the idea that standards promote trade by removing the barriers of national practice. If we equate trade with the production and exchange of bibliographic records, we can immediately see the impact that common standards have made within the Anglo-American library tradition and elsewhere. For the last 150 years, we have seen a progressive movement towards the adoption of common standards in bibliographic record creation. This has been particularly strongly marked in the sphere of cataloguing, where the introduction of the ISBD and the second edition of the Anglo-American Cataloguing Rules have led to catalogues which, at the level of bibliographic description of the physical manifestation of a work, are not only internally consistent within a single library, but between libraries nationally and internationally. As time goes on our international stockpile of such records grows, for both newly catalogued material and retrospectively converted catalogue records which follow these same standards. The enormous value of this resource in facilitating systematic access to the content of our collections must not be allowed to be underestimated.

'Standards are important for any industry because they increase the market size.'[6] This quotation from an article concerning standards in the manufacture of CD-ROM discs shows that in assessing and evaluating standards for bibliographic control in the same terms as standards in any other commercial market, we must make the case that not only do standards promote trade but their use increases the market size for the buying and selling of records. Standards promote growth, and it is abundantly clear that internationally used bibliographic standards have induced substantial growth in the market for bibliographic records. An industry where a lack of standards initially inhibited growth, the video industry, serves as a useful reminder of the commercial perils of a lack of standardization. The video market originally witnessed a battle to establish the supremacy of videodiscs or videotapes, which was no sooner won by videotapes than a second battle broke out between the VHS and the Beta tape formats. It was only when the VHS format finally became established as the used standard that the market really took off.

We have simple standards for bibliographic description, but for the provision of vocabulary-controlled name and title access to intellectual content the picture is not as clear. AACR2 certainly gives us rules for creating standard forms of name and uniform title, but the actual data content of those controlled names and titles may well legitimately vary from catalogue to catalogue, depending on the coverage of the collection and the requirements of its users. To enable removal of the barriers to international bibliographic record exchange, a standard set of cataloguing rules is simply not enough. The next great step forward is to achieve common use of a standard bibliographic tool in the shape of a common authority file.

At the national level, there has been some progress towards this already. The British Library has made available its Name Authority List since 1981. Originally including only name headings generated by the copyright items recorded in the British National Bibliography, the Name Authority List now contains headings originating from other parts of the British Library collections, as the BL moves towards a common system of authority control across its major catalogues. The five other copyright libraries, who now share the task of recording the national copyright output, also contribute headings to the Name Authority List as part of that process. However, at the same time as we have been moving towards the development of a distributed national level authority file, the growth in international record exchange, particularly through facilities and institutions in the United States, has brought us up short against the fact that the headings on records emanating from the major North American institutions and facilities are created in the context of the United States national authority file. This means that, internationally, British records are not as effective as they could be for US libraries, and US records are not as effective as they could be in our British catalogues. We are not meeting the needs of the market, and we are not penetrating the largest market of all, that of the United States.

The obvious solution is to use a common authority file. As we found with the introduction of AACR2, however, libraries are highly resistant to anything that involves change to their catalogues, and – as the hinge on which the door of systematic access swings – changes to access points are a particularly sensitive area. We all want the benefits of cooperation, and we want them for free. But nothing comes free in the market economy. However, the option of continuing to operate under a fortress library mentality has run out, just as has the option to operate an isolationist, 'Little England' economic policy. To their great credit the two national libraries, the Library of Congress and the British Library, have made the choice to converge their cataloguing policies for their mutual long term benefit and for the benefit of all libraries using BL and LC records in their catalogues. The first fruit of this cooperation will be the Anglo-American Authority File; a name and title authority file used in common by both national libraries, and by all those libraries elsewhere which choose to accept the common policies used in its creation and maintenance.

For the British Library, this is a major strategic development which will involve substantial short-term change in its own catalogues and services. The BL has negotiated a cataloguing policy convergence agreement with the Library of Congress, which will be operational for all new authority headings created. The common authority file will be loaded into the BL's automated systems, and the massive job of bringing its catalogues into line with the AAAF will commence. These changes to both policies and catalogues will be neither cheap nor easy, and, because it must maintain systematic access to its collections, cannot be either quick or dirty – but for the British Library as a major record creation agency, for libraries taking its records into their catalogues, and for the catalogue users themselves, the long term benefits will be enormous. As just one example, the 'hit rate' from the AAAF for headings needed in original cataloguing will rise with the expansion of the pool of existing authority records from which we can draw. That means that libraries will have to expend less cataloguer resource in new authority record creation. Similarly, when a library uses copy cataloguing from any other library whose records contain headings selected from the common authority file, it will no longer have to invest cataloguer resource in checking and changing the headings in the record against a separate British Library authority file. These are resource savings that will be matched by the enhanced utility of British records in the North American and Australasian markets.

From the descriptive cataloguing point of view the trade barriers are coming down. Subject cataloguing has never been aligned on a single international standard, for sound practical and professional reasons. In providing subject access to, and organization of, its resources, a library is completely focused on the requirements of its user community in the way it approaches subject analysis of its collection. In choosing a classification scheme, for example, a library is likely to select one of the main contenders – the Dewey Decimal Classification, or the Library of Congress Classification, or maybe the Universal Decimal Classification – but the fact remains that as long as different user communities have different subject access requirements there is no prospect of these main contenders producing a single winner. Naturally, bibliographic record exchange is limited if the record you are selling does not have a classification number from the scheme used by the library seeking to buy, and you are less likely to buy a record which does not have a number from your library's classification scheme.

In the field of subject headings there has been progress. The British Library has for many years used subject indexing schemes which have been developed in-house – PRECIS, and more recently the son of PRECIS, COMPASS. These schemes have not been successful in attracting new users, and indeed have not been used consistently or comprehensively even within the British Library itself. This failure to penetrate the subject headings market has meant that the BL as a record producer now finds itself in a difficult position in seeking to sell. If it wants its records to be more attractive in the market, it needs to provide subject headings which are in demand. From its viewpoint as a record buyer, if the British Library wants to provide its users with vocabulary-controlled subject access which meets their needs, but at the same time wants to cut its cataloguing costs by making more use of copy cataloguing, it is going to have to make use of a subject headings scheme found on a high percentage of those source copy cataloguing records. To enhance its position as both a buyer and a seller in the bibliographic market, the British Library has recently reintroduced Library of Congress Subject Headings to the records it provides for the British National Bibliography. Not only that, but it is planning to extend the use of LCSH as widely as possible within the BL itself, so that for the first time in its history there is the genuine prospect of consistent subject access to the BL collections. This is a truly major step forward in providing quality access to users of the British Library catalogues and collections.

Protecting the consumer

Now let us look at the way in which standards 'protect consumer interests through adequate and consistent quality of goods and services'. The consumer interest the librarian must constantly have in mind is the satisfaction of the knowledge and information needs of the community through the best possible use of the contents of the collection funded by that community. We are the guardians of a community asset, and we must exercise our professional skills and understanding to make the best possible use of that asset. Consistency is a critical quality in the application of bibliographic standards. Our organizational and access systems are of value because they are predictable, and they continue to be predictable only if they are consistently applied.

One of the great achievements of AACR2 is the consistent bibliographic analysis of all media. Because of its coverage of all media, AACR has found itself able to respond to new technological developments without disturbing the underlying principles on which it is built. Put simply, these principles enable the combination in a single record of a description of the bibliographic item with access points to the intellectual content of that item. These principles have been more or less adhered to by British cataloguers. In North America, however, there has been some muddying of the waters, and a certain lack of rigour in separating the physical manifestation and the intellectual content of a knowledge record. Given the play *Hamlet* on microfiche, the Library of Congress Rule Interpretations 'interpret' AACR so as to produce a description, not of the microfiche, but of the original printed manifestation which is displayed on the microfiche. It may be that this confusion between access to the work and access to the differing manifestations of that work has fuelled the fire currently raging over AACR2's ability to catalogue electronic documents. The lack of a 'physical' item to describe is held to undermine one of AACR's cardinal principles, as defined in rule 0.24 – a principle which has already been undermined in the LCRI treatment of microreproductions. To the practical and pragmatic British this seems an unnecessarily confused approach to the principles of the rules and their application.

Electronic documents do exist in physical form, even though they cannot be picked up and looked at. AACR has a chapter dealing with the cataloguing of computer files, which is exactly what such electronic documents are.

To meet the North American demand for enhancement of the AACR rules to catalogue electronic media, OCLC produced guidelines based on the results of a project involving extensive groundwork by a number of volunteer participating libraries. These Guidelines were subsequently examined by an American Library Association Task Force, with a view to producing proposals for rule revision of AACR wherever this was deemed necessary. It has been instructive to find that the revision proposals which have followed from the report of the Task Force have been minor, both in extent and intent.

The need for consistency in order to safeguard consumer interests counsels against undue and unnecessary changes to standards. It is only during the last 15 years that we have had a period of real stability in our cataloguing code. There are still a great many catalogues in use which conform to earlier standards and tools. We are not just talking here of differences in physical medium, although of course there are many catalogues extant on card, fiche, and even in print. The much more serious difficulty from the point of view of providing comprehensive systematic access to a collection is a lack of bibliographic integration of these separate catalogues. The British Library Catalogue of Printed Books, for example, has been successfully converted to computer-readable form, but it is still not possible to search that catalogue and the catalogues of more recent material acquired by the British Library as a bibliographic whole. The most telling difference is in the form of access points. Each catalogue is internally consistent – the British Library Catalogue to a much greater extent than the online catalogue of current humanities and social sciences material, which has been extremely poorly controlled in the past – but the form of heading for the same bibliographic identity may well vary between these internally consistent catalogues. A comprehensive retrospective bibliographic search cannot rely on automated sources alone, because not all sources have been automated – but it also cannot rely on the consistency of bibliographic data whatever the source medium may be. The longer the period of stability for AACR, the greater the stock of records produced to consistent standards and the better our users will be served.

Standards bring savings

The third element in our definition of standards is 'to promote economy in human effort, materials and energy in the production and exchange of goods'. In cataloguing terms, we are talking here about cooperation. Cooperation in catalogue record production is an idea that has been propagated for many years, but in this country there have been few genuinely participative projects. It is not entirely clear why this is the case, although I would hazard a guess that public libraries have, by and large, been all but entirely drawn into the bibliographic utilities and now function almost exclusively as buyers in the bibliographic market. Original cataloguing seems a dying art in the public libraries – a far cry from the Golden Age of British cataloguing, when many of its most original and innovative thinkers had a public library background which led to fresh ideas and insights. In the large academic and research libraries, and I would include the British Library in this criticism, there has been a persistent fortress library mentality which until very recently has been extremely difficult to pierce. There is a well-known joke in the United States which says that cataloguers believe only two libraries produce good quality cataloguing – their own and the Library of Congress. For large British academic libraries, you can forget the Library of Congress! In academia change has been seen as for the worse, and costly to boot, and the larger the catalogue and the larger the collection, the more costly change becomes.

The pincer movement of increasing automation and decreasing funds has pushed academic and research libraries, albeit with a certain degree of reluctance, into each others arms. Even now, however, the full benefits of cooperation are being denied to users and libraries alike. Automation has made it easy and relatively cheap for libraries to combine their catalogues into a single database, giving them a pool of records from which to draw for their own purposes. But they still will not make the changes to their application policies which would turn this as yet murky pool, suitable only for simplistic known-information and specific-item searches, into a genuinely valuable means of access to the combined intellectual content of these libraries' collections and at the same time make more effective use of their own resources. True cooperative projects demand common standards, common tools, and common application policies. They are, in the end, a means to the end of better serving our user communities, not better serving ourselves.

Another development which is taking place as cooperative programmes mushroom is the definition of a 'core record'. This is an agreed minimum set of bibliographic data for a catalogue record which every library participating in a cooperative programme commits to provide, thereby ensuring maximum flexibility in the subsequent use of the record across a wide range of library catalogues. The core record, like the common authority file, is an application standard and, like the authority file, it generates consistency of product amongst record creation agencies. The problem of lack of a single, standard, classification scheme is usually met by an obligation on the participants to provide a classification number from at least one of the major classification schemes in the core record.

So far we have considered the market in bibliographic records and the standards which are used to describe bibliographic items and give access to their intellectual content. Libraries also operate as buyers in a much wider market, that for carriers of recorded knowledge such as books, sound recordings, videotapes and electronic documents and databases. Standards also exist which promote economy and efficiency in the supply of library materials. The value of a unique identifier for single carriers of recorded knowledge has been recognized in the development of the ISBN, the ISSN and now also the ISRN for reports, the ISRC for musical recordings and the ISMN for printed music. These standards mark the point in the information chain at which the needs of the suppliers of recorded knowledge and the demands of libraries acquiring recorded knowledge converge. These standards relate solely to the bibliographic item (usually, but not always, a single physical entity) and are basically single-functional, that is, they are concerned with the control of information relating to the item and not with the control of its content, the intellectual work which it carries.

The ISSN is an international standard (ISO 3297). The ISSN system is administered by the ISSN International Centre, located in Paris, which acts as the registration authority for ISSN by maintaining a worldwide register of serial publications. The register lists all the ISSNs allocated, together with their accompanying bibliographic record, and is in effect a bibliography of serials. Radiating out from the International Centre are a number of national centres, each responsible for registering the serial publications of its country. Many attempts have been made to combine production of the serial record for the ISSN system with that for the library catalogue, usually with only limited success.

The ISBN has a longer history and has not attempted to tie itself to any specifically defined form of bibliographic record. Like the ISSN, the ISBN is used in all three sectors of the book industry – publishers, the book trade, and libraries – and again, like the ISSN, it is the first two groups, concerned solely with the supply and control of physical stock, which have been able to benefit most from its use. The ISBN is the key to a specific title. It stands as a surrogate for the title in ordering and stock control functions, minimizing problems of transcription and language in the supply process. The library functions which find most use for ISBNs and ISSNs are acquisitions, circulation and interlending, again all functions tied to the supply and demand of physical items. Cataloguers benefit from the ISBN and ISSN when they are engaged in the supply and demand of bibliographic records for their catalogues. Searching by ISBN or ISSN is an effective way of locating a record for a specific known item in a catalogue or database; the record can then be used in retrospective conversion programmes, copy cataloguing, or, by library users, in the information retrieval process.

Finally, a look at the standard used to communicate the vast majority of computer-readable catalogue records. We store these bibliographic records in a format – the MARC format – which was originally derived from the structure of the entries in a card catalogue. If it were possible to choose one single standard to undergo root and branch reform, many would choose the MARC format.

Strangely, it is far less liberal and democratic in its openness to change than any of the major cataloguing or classification standards. The MARC format needs to be revised to take account of the possibilities of the developed automated catalogue environment, and specifically to allow the representation of multi-dimensional records which reflect true bibliographic relationships. We can define within the bibliographic information system a nested sequence of series-monograph-analytical which is capable of portrayal only in a very rudimentary fashion in the MARC format. This multi-dimensional information system consists of the vocabulary-controlled points of access to intellectual works, the descriptions of the manifestations of intellectual works, and a linkage mechanism between these two layers. The MARC format, in its parody of the two-dimensional catalogue card, perpetuates the muddying of the distinction, quite clearly made in the cataloguing code itself, between intellectual work and physical manifestation.

If we are to make economies, MARC formats, like authority files, need to be shared amongst as many participants in the production and exchange of bibliographic records as is possible. Steps are now being taken by the national libraries of Great Britain, the United States and Canada to align the UKMARC, USMARC and CANMARC formats. As in all other fields of bibliographic control, national standards that once fulfilled a useful purpose in pulling together and enhancing the national cataloguing output, are now seen as impeding trade in the global bibliographic economy. The National Library of Australia, in consultation with the Australian library community, is going one step beyond alignment and is allowing AUSMARC gradually to be replaced by USMARC. It is interesting that the National Library of Australia, in initiating consultation on the future of AUSMARC, went to great lengths to ensure that the response it got came from 'a senior management perspective'.[7] The decision on the future of AUSMARC was taken on a primarily long-term economic rationale, affected as little as possible by chauvinistic or insular debate or the short-term concerns of cataloguers or systems librarians.

In an article written 15 years ago at the time of the introduction of AACR2, Michael Gorman said 'the door to bibliographic progress is turning on the hinge of mechanisation and standardisation'.[8] Both continue to go hand in hand, now as then. The standardization and centralization of bibliographic information continue as goals for the current suppliers to the bibliographic market. Standards, including descriptive cataloguing codes, lists of verbal subject descriptions and classification schemes, all emanate from a central authority, usually a major player or consortium of major players in the bibliographic market, and are intended for national and international use through networking and other cooperative bibliographic projects. 'The development of standards such as AACR2, ISBD, and MARC format has proven that cataloging is a science in which standardization and consistency are a necessity. The large amount of heuristics possessed by expert catalogers suggests that cataloging is also an art where judgement and creativity play important roles'.[9] How that interesting marriage of art and science can most effectively and economically be consummated is the subject of the next chapters. We now need to look at the way in which catalogue records are created and supplied, and how a healthy bibliographic market can best tend to the common good.

References

1   Monbiot, George, 'Global villagers speak with forked tongues', *Guardian*, 24 August 1995, 13.

2   Law, Derek, 'How microwaved is your poodle?', *Catalogue & index*, (114), Winter 1994, 1–6.

3   Eco, Umberto, 'The texts to boot', *Observer review*, 18 June 1995, 4.

4   Bourne, Ross, 'Standards: who needs them?', *Library Association record*, 96 (3), March 1994, 149.

5   Ward, Sandra, 'Standards: their relevance to scientific and technical information', *Aslib proceedings*, 46 (1), January 1994, 4.

6   Pahwa, Ash, 'When can a standard be a "real" standard?', *CD-ROM professional*, 7 (5), September/October 1994, 112–4.

7   McMillan, Simon, 'AUSMARC to US MARC', *Cataloguing Australia*, 17 (3/4), September/December 1991, 113–9.

8   Gorman, Michael, 'The prospective catalog', in *Closing the catalog*, London, Oryx Press, 1980.

---

9 Jeng, Ling Hwey, 'The structure of a knowledge base for cataloging rules', *Information processing and management*, 27 (1), 1991,
   109.

CHAPTER 6
CATALOGUING TODAY

Cataloguing is an activity in which librarians use information to help create information about still other information. The information we use is found in our descriptive cataloguing rules, subject cataloguing rules, classification schemes, application policies, and formats and files of all sorts. The information we create is placed in authority records and catalogue records. Finally, the whole process itself revolves round the information in books, documents, manuscripts, databases, sound recordings, videos, pictures and all the other carriers of knowledge in our library collections.

The art of cataloguing lies in creatively bringing together the scientific, analytic approach of the bibliographic standards and the interpretative gloss of the application policies, within the frame of the bibliographic information to hand. To practise their art at its highest levels cataloguers need to develop both professional and technological expertise, and they need to be able to communicate the results of that expertise effectively through the medium of the catalogue. Their skills are applied in searching bibliographic databases, determining vocabulary controlled access points, interpreting bibliographic data, and the rules for processing that bibliographic data, and above all in identifying and prioritizing problems or special cases. We have seen that the organization and use of a collection demand standards, and now, in their turn, standards demand consistency of application if the library is to exploit fully its collection for the benefit of its user community. In this chapter we are concerned with the application of standards, tools and policies in the cataloguing process, and with the difficulties we meet in managing that cataloguing process today.

Currency and coverage

If the catalogue is going to successfully meet the needs of its user community, the manager who takes responsibility for the cataloguing process must constantly keep two objectives in mind: currency and coverage. Unless a record is there in the catalogue at the time the user searches for information, the information for which the record acts as a surrogate is lost to the user and the collection is not used effectively. Users take it for granted that the collection is fully represented by the catalogue. Online catalogues are widely held, not only to have increased the demands users make on the collection, but also to have raised their expectations of what might be found in it. It is also evident that users view the results of a computer catalogue search far less sceptically than those they might obtain through a print or fiche product. The flexible search patterns made possible by the computer, particularly the ability to keyword search, make it more than likely that the user will retrieve *something* – even from the most poorly organized catalogue – and mistakenly assume he or she has retrieved everything the collection has to offer. Heightened user beliefs and expectations from the automated catalogue make it more important than ever that the cataloguing manager strives to provide optimum levels of currency and coverage.

In this endeavour to provide currency and coverage in the catalogue, questions of what the library should catalogue and how, when, and at what level of detail, have to be continuously at the forefront of the mind of every cataloguing manager. They are faced on a daily basis with the difficult task of balancing the information needs of the community against the means and resources available through the catalogue to meet those needs. To what level of detail should a work be analysed? Should the library record individual journal articles, for example, and if so, should this be a comprehensive policy for all serials, for the most frequently used serials, or for those in certain subject fields? Is it necessary to include authority-controlled headings in all catalogue records, or will keyword searching alone be sufficient to meet access requirements for some categories of material? Is a non-standard record really better than no record at all?

Although its substance results from cataloguer analysis of the intellectual work carried in an item, the catalogue record will also include data and information about the individual physical carrier itself. Catalogues traditionally bring together data relating to both the content of the work, for the benefit of the user, and the item, for the benefit of the librarian. This 'housekeeping' information enables the librarian to keep track of the physical location of the item – whether it is on loan or perhaps being repaired. The creation and maintenance of such data often, although not always, falls to the cataloguer. At the very least the cataloguing manager will be responsible for the effective integration of the data relating to both the work and the physical piece, so that the library's access system operates efficiently and with a due regard to the security and preservation of the library's resources.

The means and resources available to carry out the cataloguing process never exist in a state of stasis. Decisions need to be taken, but they also need to be constantly open to re-evaluation in the light of current options and possibilities – always keeping in sight the twin cataloguing goals of currency and coverage.

Cover what you have to cover

The average user, and perhaps even the average librarian, assumes that the catalogue is the sole access route to all the information in the collection – or if it isn't then it should be. The cacophony of criticism flying in the direction of cataloguers for their failure to 'catalogue the Internet' is built on this facile assumption. Of course, the catalogue is not, never has been and never will be, the sole means of access to the contents of a collection. At the level of the physical item, material recently purchased by the library, but not yet catalogued, may be recorded in a variety of acquisitions files. Material acquired through purchase, gift or exchange, and sitting in backlogs, is often inaccessible physically or intellectually. Information relating to this uncatalogued physical collection may be available to staff, but is rarely so to the public. At another level of information we have what we might call 'carrier' bibliographic items – serials, encyclopaedias, databases or other compilations of works or data. The catalogue provides access to the bibliographic carrier, but not to the individual works, information or data carried. Finally, of course, there is a whole wealth of material which, although not owned by the library, is available to it remotely, or by copy or loan, from another source.

Searching a remote database and downloading an electronic text is, in essence, no different in kind from any other form of interlibrary lending. It may well be quicker and it does not entail the risk of the item already being on loan elsewhere, but there are other aspects of the transaction which can make loan, or photocopying, a preferable option. As always, the library has to balance user needs with available resources. There should be no question of recording copied or downloaded works in the receiving library's catalogue unless and until the work becomes a permanent part of the collection in some form. The catalogue of a library should record the resources of the library, just as the index of an archive of photographs should cover the photographs in the archive, and a computer database of documents or other material for remote search and retrieval should be organized, recorded and indexed by the institution making the database available.

The lack of a single source for information about the collection is of course a barrier to coherent and effective searching – but the picture gets still darker. Even the less than comprehensive coverage of the catalogue is qualitatively worsened by the fact that the catalogue rarely exists as one integrated bibliographic entity. Rules change, and the media in which catalogues are held change. Automated catalogues have now established near-universal supremacy, and retrospective conversion programmes are slowly pulling together catalogues within the confines of this single medium. But there are still problems of bibliographic integration within the single computer catalogue as different categories of records continue to reflect the chronological strata of changing cataloguing standards and policies.

Scattering of information is a barrier to the user, but it is a barrier which has been recognized and a barrier which can be surmounted. Catalogues have, in fact, developed in a way which has tried not to duplicate those avenues of access to information available elsewhere. As we have seen, catalogues in general do not dig far below the whole-item level, either because that information is available through separate indexes or because the carrier work itself is organized to provide such analytical access through an integrated index or an alphabetical, numerical or other linear structure. Catalogues are just one among many means of access to information, some parts of which are organized, some of which are not. It is imprudent and unnecessary to suggest, as some now do, that catalogues should give access to information they are not best placed to provide, to which they will not be the natural means of access, and certainly which they are not resourced to provide.

What are we paying for?

It is a truth universally acknowledged by cataloguers that the value of a bibliographic record is directly related to the rigour and consistency with which standards are applied during its creation. It is an equally commonly held belief of library administrators that the cost of a catalogue record is so high because these same standards encourage the nit-picking, perfectionist proclivities of cataloguers. Both views blur reality. The high-quality organization of knowledge and access to information all librarians desire is possible only through the consistent application of standards, but cataloguers all too frequently confuse the letter of the rule interpretation with the spirit of its principle. Perfection is a legitimate and laudable aim for a cataloguer, but we have to teach in what perfection lies. Much of the consistency of application on which cataloguers pride themselves is based on a knowledge of rule interpretations and policies which were once necessary but have long passed their sell-by date in the light of developments in the media in which catalogues are held and searched and the means by which records are created and obtained.

The 'unit record' is one important example of the way in which cataloguers have used the possibilities of automation to make economies while at the same time enhancing systematic access to the collection. The unit record consists of a bibliographic description of the carrier and vocabulary-controlled access points appropriate to the work carried and its physical manifestation. This single record replaces the full 'main entry' and the abbreviated 'added entries' of the printed catalogue and the early card catalogue. The automated authority file is another development which has married an intellectual process for adding value with the possibilities of computer systems to deliver enhanced performance from the catalogue and the collection. The authority file consists of authority records, each containing the authorized, controlled form of heading used in the catalogue together with all other forms of the name or title or subject which a user might reasonably use in a search for material related to that name, title or subject. To function most effectively, the authority file will be linked to the online catalogue. With such automated links in place, the access point and the bibliographic description are brought together only at the point at which a search is made. The data relating to vocabulary-controlled access points is held just once, in the authority file, instead of repeatedly throughout the catalogue. Such a system produces, in its turn, further economies in catalogue maintenance costs. Should the form of an access point need to be changed, it is changed once and once only on the authority record and is immediately available in its new form across the catalogue in all the records to which that authority record is linked. The catalogue continues to fulfil its function of pulling together the records related to a heading quickly and comprehensively; at one and the same time some of the past barriers to effective catalogue searching are removed.

Automation has spread quickly and widely throughout libraries, with large sums of money being spent on the promise of saving cataloguer time and cutting the cost of cataloguing. It is almost certain, however, that automation has not significantly reduced the time necessary to create an original cataloguing record. In 1974 the number of copyright items catalogued by a professional member of staff working for the British National Bibliography, completing a catalogue form by hand and checking authority headings in a card file, averaged about 20 per day; 20 years later a British Library cataloguer using an automated system and an online authority file creates pretty much the same number.

At the Library of Congress, the staff costs of cataloguing a single item are about $50.[1] At the British Library, the unit cost per catalogue record is somewhere between £5 and £30, depending on where in the Library the record was created, how, and for what purpose. There is of course no standard way of producing unit costs and comparisons between organizations are certainly not odorous. The lesson which can be learnt very rapidly from the failure to significantly reduce the amount of time it takes to produce a catalogue record is that we cannot make significant savings from enhanced individual performance. The unit cost of cataloguing should not be based on original cataloguing alone, and neither should the cost of cataloguing an item from scratch be taken in isolation from the percentage of cataloguing the organization obtains from elsewhere and the amount of editorial intervention then expended on this copy cataloguing. Savings can be achieved by managing the cataloguing process so as to maximize the benefits of cooperative cataloguing and minimize the amount of necessary change to records taken into the catalogue from elsewhere. We save by demanding more from the process rather than demanding more from the individual.

Cutting the cost

In its insistence that an item be catalogued once and once only, and the resulting record be used as widely as possible, the principle of Universal Bibliographic Control has long stood as a beacon for economy in record creation. Pragmatic considerations are now moving us rapidly towards practical fulfilment of the theory. Despite the stark simplicity and idealism of the principle, it demands prudence and a hard-headed business sense in its application – the responsibility for creating that 'once and for all' record has to be shared as widely as possible, and the record has to be of a quality to fit it for its purpose.

Always jumping on the bandwagons others are jumping off, library administrators now believe that computers, not catalogues, make libraries work. Just when professionals in the IT field are discovering all those effective gadgets in libraries which provide a quality of retrieval undreamt of by database software alone, library administrators are anxious to dump their expensive cataloguers and buy in catalogue records from outside. We have, of course, been buying in catalogue records for many years. What was a BNB card but outsourced record creation? With the growth of a market in catalogue records, however, the question is no longer 'Who will provide the best-quality cataloguing for my library?', but 'How much quality can my library afford?'. The public funding given to the British Library to provide a national bibliography for the country's libraries is being eroded, but its legal obligation to do so remains. The British Library has continually to find new ways to fulfil its obligations to provide catalogue records to the library community, within the context of continual government questioning of its own role in catalogue record creation.

This is a matter of concern to all those libraries that have benefited from the quality of cataloguing which the BL has been resourced to provide in the past. Cataloguing from the Library of Congress and the British Library and from other major research libraries has meant cataloguing from experts, backed up with resources of scale. Now that catalogue records are available from a variety of computer networks and databases, local libraries have been given the prerogative of choice – the elemental justification for introducing the market. But choice exercised in favour of lower quality records can lead only to the demise of high-quality record providers and the final eradication of bibliographic and subject expertise.

There is an ever-increasing dependence on shared cataloguing throughout the international library community as even libraries in the Premier League have discovered that it is not possible to produce original, in-house cataloguing for all the items joining their collections. A natural product of any increase in copy cataloguing is a decline in original cataloguing. In some larger libraries the decline will be in percentage rather than real terms. The volume of 'special collections' acquisitions may still stretch the resources of the library to produce original copy, irrespective of any growth in the availability of copy cataloguing for more general materials. Nonetheless, it would be difficult to discover a library that is doing more original cataloguing than it was ten or even five years ago.

Cutting the length

The availability of copy cataloguing varies according to the material being catalogued. The British Library finds records for about

50% of the material catalogued by its general cataloguing teams; a
survey of BLCMP libraries discovered that a record was available
on the BLCMP databases for about 90% of items, and 80% of these
records were usable without editing.[2] The large international bibliographic utilities such as OCLC and RLIN, together with smaller
national utilities like BLCMP, are well established as the principal
suppliers of machine-readable catalogue records for books and serials. All the major sources of original cataloguing, including the
Library of Congress and the British Library, feed records to these
bibliographic utilities. The development of the utilities from suppliers of individual bibliographic records to suppliers of entire bibliographic systems and services is a pointer to the future. Their
increasing emphasis on authority control systems is an indication
that they now set their sights much higher than the supply of individual records and simplistic 'known record' searching of their
databases, and aim to answer the complexities of subject and work
title searches – searches which can be met only by the systematic
presentation and rigorous control of data. In adopting common
integrative tools and standards, the databases have become catalogues, but catalogues which are not tied to any specific collection.
By using the same tools and standards, catalogues for individual
libraries can be built from the records in the utility databases with
a minimum of editorial intervention. In essence, we have an embry-
onic global information system at the level of the distinct bibliographic carrier, into which each individual library can feed and
from which each individual library can be fed.

Matching this process, library catalogues are increasingly being
linked to each other, merged to provide databases such as that of
Consortium of University Research Libraries (CURL), or made
available for standalone remote searching. All these developments
use common technical standards, but by no means the same attention has been paid to ensuring that the cataloguing data in the
linked or merged or standalone catalogues is capable of bibliographic integration. Only when a user can take a vocabulary-controlled heading and retrieve relevant material from all the linked or
merged catalogues, or take a heading used in a remote search of
one library online public access catalogue (OPAC) and use it, suc-

cessfully, in another, will we come anywhere near fulfilling the true potential of these developments. The use of common standards, common bibliographic tools, and common application policies is not only an economic necessity for cataloguing departments; it also leads to vitally enhanced access for the user and far more effective use of all collections. Each individual catalogue has to be seen as a building block in a larger national and international system of access to information.

During the resource-hungry 1980s, with their ever-tightening restraints on staff resources and constant pressure to justify expenditure, serious attention was paid on both sides of the Atlantic to the concept of 'minimal-level cataloguing'. Wishing to meet the need to provide access to the material it owned through a catalogue record with the smallest possible amount of bibliographic detail, libraries attempted to discover of what this minimum set of data consisted.

Minimal-level cataloguing is, by its very definition, less informative than full cataloguing. This does not present problems to the searcher, as long as the known information concerning the work, subject or item in which he or she is interested matches that placed in the catalogue record. A search for a known title, even one recalled with less than total accuracy, may still be successful using a minimal-level record. Even here, though, success can depend on factors that are difficult to control or counteract, within the confines of a brief record requiring little bibliographic checking on the part of the cataloguer. In a large catalogue, many records may contain common title words, leading to retrieval of uncomfortably large numbers of postings. The lack of data in the record to assist in further refining the search may well mean that a useful item is missed through an *embarras de richesse*.

To calm the fears of cataloguers and catalogue users concerned that minimal catalogue records would diminish access to the collection, minimal-level records were justified to posterity as being only a temporary expedient. The records would, in the fullness of time, be upgraded – if not by the originating library, then by someone else. The reality is that once a less than full record is created, particularly one from a reliable source, there it will stay in the catalogue. Less than full records can indeed work in a catalogue, but by and large there are no second chances if we fail to get it right first time.

Yet still the backlogs grow ...

In spite of shared cataloguing and minimal-level cataloguing, backlogs, like original cataloguing, are still with us to a greater or lesser degree – and the degree is likely to be greater in specialist collecting areas. As one example, in a survey carried out in 1993 75% of responding libraries claimed to have a music cataloguing backlog.[3] The reasons given for the existence of their backlog varied from the volume of gifts and the volume of acquisition to the level of professional staff and the level of non-professional staff. The answer to the backlog was almost uniformly held to be more money to employ more cataloguers. Interestingly, few respondents felt the answer lay in a lower level of cataloguing, however that might be defined. Similar findings resulted from a more general survey carried out by Camden and Cooper in relation to a backlog at their own library at the University of Virginia.[4] They found that 77–78% of research libraries reported 'significant' backlogs, and again discovered that full cataloguing was felt to be desirable and that there were not sufficient numbers of professional cataloguers.

Studies of backlogged material have shown that it does indeed consist predominantly of items that the library is not sufficiently resourced to catalogue, but this is a question of lack of skills, not staff. The material is usually in a form, or in a language, that cataloguers are not able or qualified to handle. Whilst too much can be made of the need for cataloguers to be expert in the subject matter they are cataloguing, certainly lack of facility in a language can cause serious problems for the user and, where mistakes occur, diminish use of the collection – if not the amusement factor in the catalogue. We are probably all acquainted with characters such as the well-known Welsh writer, Gruffud Hiraethog Gwaith.

Earlier chapters considered the debate concerning access or ownership. Whilst it is indisputable that ownership of a work is the quickest and surest means of offering access to its contents, this can be true only if a bibliographic record is present in the catalogue to enable that access. A library may be proud of the scope and scale of its collections and the variety of media it provides, but these are nothing other than window-dressing unless their content can be discovered and used by the community. Backlogs of uncatalogued material vitiate ownership of that material. Acquisitions budgets and cataloguing budgets must run in parallel. Increased investment in library holdings and the provision of remotely held information will be wasted unless at the same time there is equivalent investment in the provision of access to these materials – how can a library seriously contemplate purchasing material which it does not equally plan to provide the resources to catalogue? Unfortunately, we have been unable to convince library administrators that providing access means much more than enabling keyword searching of titles, a function which the computer is conveniently placed to carry out. Hidden beneath this blithe abdication of our professional responsibilities to the user community, though, is the fact that even the quality of keyword access is entirely dependent on the content and structure of the database of bibliographic information fuelling the keyword search. Providing access to content has to be the primary motivator for any cataloguer. The cataloguing manager must harness that motivation by planning and utilizing resources so as minimize backlogs and maximize systematic access.

Streamlining the process

The need to minimize backlogs is just one consideration among many when organizing the cataloguing process for optimum catalogue currency and coverage at minimum cost. Most cataloguing departments rightly prioritize material on the basis of the needs of the users of the collection. A kind of inverse, unofficial prioritization also operates, however, based on cataloguer likes and dislikes, their subject strengths and weaknesses, and the perceived complexity of the material with which they are faced. We have seen that foreign-language and specialist materials, feature heavily in backlogs. There is also evidence that material on scientific subjects, despite its propensity to age more quickly than social science or humanities items, spends longer in the cataloguing process.[5] A vicious circle exists which is difficult to break: many cataloguers lack interest and expertise in handling scientific material, therefore

----

it remains uncatalogued, with the result that few libraries make available copy cataloguing to ease the problem for others.

Concentration by cataloguers on an item-by-item record creation or record sourcing process can blinker them to many of the most important demands of an organized system of access. Increasingly they focus on the unit production of catalogue records, which they either create themselves or search a bibliographic database to find. Cataloguers, just like many library users, have become engaged solely in 'known item' searching, although in their case the sought item is a bibliographic record rather than a book, tape or other carrier of information. Once the record is created or found, downloaded, and edited, the computer takes it and feeds it into the catalogue. Not only are cataloguers isolated from the users, they are also increasingly isolated from the catalogue itself as an intellectually coherent entity. The greater this isolation becomes, the greater the likelihood that cataloguers will lose their understanding of how the catalogue records interact with the classified collection and with other avenues of access to information available in the library. Record creation by computer presents further evidence of the current obsession with the single unit at the expense of the group: the individual rather than the community; the known-item search rather than structured browsing; the piece of information rather than the mass of knowledge; the specific case rather than the body of principles.

The card catalogue, by its very nature, exacerbated this unit-of-production mentality by reinforcing the conception that the physical item and the catalogue record were equivalent. Each separate physical item that the library acquired was matched by its own separate physical card surrogate in the catalogue. Of course, certain things didn't quite fit the pattern: a serial didn't have a separate card for each physical issue, and a work appearing in several volumes probably didn't have a separate card for each individual volume. Still, the focus of the catalogue was squarely on the physical items in the collection. In the book catalogue, conversely, entries usually represented works. The printed *British Library Catalogue*, for example, heads each entry with the name of the work, and follows this with an indented list of each separate physical manifestation of the work to be found in the Library. The catalogue card, and the MARC unit record to which it gave birth, do in theory keep to this pattern by giving both a uniform title for the work followed by the title of the manifestation wherever the two are not identical, but the physical form of the catalogue card and its two-dimensional nature have effectively obscured the differing functions of the work title and the manifestation title. Any future linked-information system will, I believe, be constructed on the building block of the work rather than the physical manifestation, and it is important that we encourage cataloguers to be conscious of the difference between the two.

Such qualities as wear well

If we are creating a catalogue record that will in effect act as the means of access to information, not just in our own catalogue but potentially in an infinite number of catalogues worldwide, the record must be of a quality to fit it for its purpose and of a quality to wear well. A widely recognized spin-off from the growth of networked catalogues and shared databases is the much greater visibility of the cataloguing output of participating libraries. This results in an assessment of the quality and consistency of the work of each participant by the others.

The quality of output depends, of course, on the quality of input coming from the applied skills and values of those producing the catalogue record. In the eyes of many people (including some of those actually doing it) cataloguing is little more than copying information from a variety of sources. Those aspiring to street cred might possibly enhance the allure of the whole thing by the cataloguers' equivalent of rapping – talking MARC. In fact the organization of knowledge in libraries demands that cataloguers not only know when and how they must apply rules to specific data in a bibliographic item, but more importantly also have the professional knowledge and skills to interpret that data and to make judgements as to how the record they create will best be integrated into the library's system of access to the collection. Yes, transcription is involved – legitimately involved, as what actually appears on the item and what actually appears on the authority file is likely to inform the way in which a user searches for that item – but, critically, there are a number of decisions which must be taken regarding how information is transcribed and what vocabulary-controlled access points are added to the description of the item. These decisions must be grounded in long term training and experience. Accuracy and attention to detail are often cited as appropriate qualities for a cataloguer; consistency and quality of judgement are equally necessary in creating a system of access.

Because of its image as a mechanistic process based on the application of rules, there has been a great deal of interest in developing expert systems for cataloguing. Ambitions for such systems vary from the wish to feed a title page in at one end and wait for the bibliographic record to come out at the other to the more realistic desire to guide the cataloguer through the cataloguing process, taking mechanical decisions wherever possible and freeing cataloguer time for the more creative and intellectual side of the job. Almost all prototype expert systems to date have focused on Chapter 21 of AACR2, 'Choice of access points'. The rules in this chapter not only indicate which vocabulary-controlled name and title access points are necessary, they also uniformly regulate which of these access points is to be regarded as the most important or 'main entry' heading. It seems strange that prototype expert systems should concentrate attention on a chapter which, in many people's eyes, has been rendered unnecessary by the unit record and by computer catalogues. Even AACR itself permits rulings on 'main entry' to be ignored where catalogues do not distinguish between main and additional access points. Nonetheless, the chapter does cover cases involving choice and is therefore particularly susceptible to algorithms and flowcharts documenting the cataloguer's decision-making process.

In the cataloguing process, the source item presents the bibliographic data elements, the bibliographic conditions. It is the job of cataloguing rules to describe the condition and prescribe the action: it is the job of the cataloguer to recognize the condition and apply the action in the context of the library, the catalogue and its users. The bibliographic record is therefore the expression of cataloguer actions resulting from cataloguer decisions. Expertise comes when the cataloguer spends less time learning how to recognize problems and more time analysing them.

Expert systems have limitations, the two most important of which are an inability to apply common-sense reasoning and the lack of an ability to learn. Cataloguers have to be able to take decisions based on visual and linguistic clues in the title page data before them. This requires not just human cognition, but human skills of interpretation as well. Much of cataloguing is an interpretative art. Machines cannot interpret, they can only act in the way they have been programmed to act when certain conditions are present. These conditions are not capable of interpretation in the light of time- and place-critical data: if the programmed condition exists, the programmed action will be taken. If an action is not universally appropriate, the computer program must cover, in advance, all specific-case conditions and their consequent action. We have been able to progress consciously from specific-case cataloguing codes to codes based on general principles; computer programs have a long way to go to reach that level of achievement.

Not for all markets

The relative decline in the volume of original cataloguing carried out in most libraries has led to a concomitant decline in the number of posts requiring professionally qualified cataloguing staff. In association with many other factors, it has also meant that there has been a serious decline of the teaching in library schools of the theory and practice of cataloguing and classification. We may, of course, merely be witnessing the effect of market forces: if there is no demand for cataloguers, naturally there is no profit to be made in producing them. Here we have but one example of the short-termism which results from applying the constrictive and limiting theory of the market to the public services. There are more users of bibliographic records than there are creators of them – just as there are many more users of computer software than creators of programs – and yet basic programming skills are still a part of any computing course. The theory and practise of the organization of knowledge are not only skills of value to those who intend to follow the craft of cataloguer; they are also foundation skills for any librarian. By teaching them, we are investing in the future health of our library service.

A recent survey of entry-level cataloguers in the United States showed the serious problems which the decline in the teaching of cataloguing in library schools is building for the future quality of organization and access to information.[6] Two-thirds of respondents felt they had not been adequately prepared for their job by their cataloguing courses at library school; they wanted more in-depth and practical experience. Who can hope effectively to facilitate the exploitation of a library collection without an appreciation and understanding of the principles of the organization of knowledge? Of course, a problem that has always been with us is the negative perception of cataloguing inculcated in new entrants by other library professionals. The necessity and worth of cataloguing is constantly questioned; the process itself is condemned as mechanistic and suffocatingly lacking in creativity by people who really should know better. It is a fact of life that many of our libraries are now administered without this sensitivity to professional values, and it is an indictment of professionals that they have often been unable to assert the vital importance of those values in the modern environment.

So do we still need it?

If you go back say 500 years, the Pope had about 400 books and his librarian was the filing system, the index, the contents list, the retrieval mechanism and most importantly of all the regulator. The Pope said what he wanted the population to see, and his librarian made sure those were the only books they saw. It was a zero serendipity world.

When the Dickensian library emerged it had an ordered filing system and realised a magic quality – serendipity. You could find what you wanted, and chance upon other things on the way.

Now leap forward to today, and go onto the Internet. This has 100% serendipity: an infinity of information, but without order. You can't find what you're looking for. It's total chaos.[7]

These are the words of Peter Cochrane, head of advanced applica-
tions and technologies at British Telecom's laboratories in East
Anglia. Urged on the one hand by our fellow 'information scien-
tists' to dump our fuddy-duddy ideas and get virtual, what do we
hear on the other hand, but an IT professional lauding the values
embodied in the 19th-century library! Which way to turn?

All things considered, we would be wise to follow the money
and pitch our case for resources round a return to those currently
fashionable values of order and decency in public life. We have to
seize every opportunity to show that cataloguers have the skills to
bring order to chaos, even in the electronic world – and that given
the means we can and will do so. But we must also be able to show
that we can manage those means and resources with prudence and
economy. Those Victorian values again!

References

1   McCallum, Sally H., 'Standards and linked online information
    systems', *Library resources and technical services*, 34 (3), July 1990,
    361.
2   Chapman, Ann, 'Up to standard?', *Journal of librarianship and
    information science*, 26 (4), 201–10.
3   MacLeod, Judy, and Lloyd, Kim, 'A study of music cataloging
    backlogs', *Library resources and technical services*, 38 (1), January
    1994, 7–15.
4   Camden, Beth Picknally, and Cooper, Jean L., 'Controlling a
    cataloging backlog', *Library resources and technical services*, 38 (1),
    January 1994, 64–71.
5   Page, Mary, and Reagor, Melinda Ann, 'Library processing
    practices by discipline', *Library resources and technical services*, 38
    (2), April 1994, 161–7.
6   Callahan, Daren, and MacLeod, Judy, 'Recruiting and retention
    revisited', *Technical services quarterly*, 11 (4), 1994, 27–43.
7   'All wired up and raring to go', *New scientist*, 5 August 1995, 30.

CHAPTER 7

COMING UP WITH THE GOODS

Although producing a high-quality product that is eminently suitable for its purpose, although international standards are in place which structure the product and ensure its consistent development, although we live in an 'Information Age' in which the means of control and provision of access to all kinds of information are avidly hunted, cataloguing is under threat. Cataloguing is too expensive, cataloguers are not efficient, computers make cataloguing unnecessary. The provision of cataloguing by outside, commercial sources is the latest, but potentially climactic, attack on the public provision of catalogue access to a collection.

From the outset we need to face the fundamental flaw in the argument proposing that the future provision of catalogues and cataloguing should be based on the operation of market forces. In a civilized society seriously committed to providing the opportunity for all its citizens, individually, to achieve their aspirations, the unfettered market cannot be allowed to operate. Let us imagine, for one moment, that catalogue records were suddenly to be priced for a market demanding a high-quality product guaranteeing comprehensive name, title and subject access to the material they represent. That cost would cover salaries commensurate with proven applied skills in the organization of information (skills which are, as we have seen, in short supply in the market-place), the care and attention needed to ensure that standards were followed and policies applied, and, of course, an element of profit for the producing library to reinvest in its record creation business (remember, we are just imagining here!). Purchasing libraries would have the choice offered to all consumers in the market. They could pay for a top-of-the-range record which guaranteed that their collections would operate at optimum efficiency, or . . . the market would provide a whole range of cheaper products.

The provision of choice is usually claimed as the defining benefit of the market. Only the free operation of the market can bring consumer choice, and choice is not only a good thing, it is a right. Every individual should have the right to be able to obtain whatever he or she desires in the free market. Who could argue with such an ambition? However, what one desires and what one is able to afford will not always be the same thing. Opportunity without ability is a barren choice. Every consumer is faced with constant compromise and change in the matter of fulfilling desires, but always in a market economy the available amount of money is the defining focus for those compromises and changes. Some libraries – one might even say most libraries – would be willing to compromise on catalogue record quality, would be willing to lose some depth or range of access, so as to be able to buy more stock, or pay its staff more, or take any one of hundreds of other consumer choice options. Choice is not just between brands, it is between products. But always, in an unregulated market, money is the basis on which choice is exercised rather than need, opportunity or ability.

However, the ability to exercise the individual right of choice also, paradoxically, limits choice for other individuals. The freedom to choose a private school, which draws away brighter, cleverer children who would help a state school prosper, means oppression for others. The freedom of one individual to spend more earned income through tax cuts means the inability to travel by train, or to enjoy the security of proper policing, or to lead a contented old age for another. The freedom to earn wealth and create jobs in the unregulated market is the increasing insecurity of those taking the jobs, the lack of investment in the future, and the dilution of quality. Those charged with making the choice will not pay for quality because they would rather spend their money in other ways. Creating a bibliographic market which offers the choice of less quality at a lower price is a double whammy. It threatens in-house, high-quality cataloguing, and it threatens the quality of access enjoyed by the community to collections for which they have paid. Above all, it threatens the future provision of both.

There is a growing market in private information services, including mass-market online information services such as CompuServe and America Online. Information services, however are not libraries. Libraries, like health and education, need an institutional support basis to prepare, interpret and deliver their service. However, unlike health and education the service provided is not unique to the individual. Books, videos, sound recordings and all the other media held by the library are reusable in perpetuity by an infinity of individuals. Libraries organize their collections and ensure that their intellectual content is accessible but, from that point, this free information lies dormant until it is used by an individual. Catalogues are the single most important part of the institutional support function. They are inextricably linked to the collections by a web of professional practice, without which the collection is unusable. Yet libraries are being asked to consider whether this vital support function can be provided more cheaply, with no diminution in quality, from outside the institution.

There is no sustainable market in high-quality, high-cost record creation, because those who may well want it could not, and by and large would not, pay for it. There is, however, a market of sorts in the competitive provision of catalogue records, many of which services survive because the high-quality records they obtain to sell are provided at less than their actual cost price by the libraries responsible for creating them. The reason for how this came to be can be found in a blend of the historically free or cheap provision of catalogue records for the nation's libraries from a central source, and a knowledge that the market is not able to support a fully-priced product. This places cataloguers in a dilemma: like many other public sector workers, they cannot expect or demand a salary appropriate to the skills they possess or the importance of the product they provide, because there is no market for what they have to sell; on the other hand, failure to continue to practice their profession or exercise their skills, whatever the conditions and whatever the financial reward, can only disadvantage further those very members of the community cataloguers wish to help achieve their aspirations. It is a dilemma which has no solution while false considerations of the market continue to dominate the actions of library administrators. Cataloguers can use many market analogies to influence library administrators to their advantage and to the advantage of library users, but the fact that their 'product' is not bought and sold on the open market can in the end only bring them face to face with the demand that they cut costs in the provision of a service which does not generate revenue. The information-rich will get richer, and the information-poor will get poorer.

Whilst subsidized production keeps the market price of catalogue records low, it is unlikely that more resources will be invested in their production. Individual catalogue records have long been provided from sources outside the library; now we are facing the growth of commercial, for-profit organizations contracting to provide an entire cataloguing service. If we want to defend and indeed further the provision of high-quality catalogue records for the public good, we have to systematically work to ensure that those libraries and cooperatives which still supply high-quality cataloguing stay in the business. One way is to ensure that our catalogues are constructed on standard principles, and that our bibliographic tools and policies follow standard international practice. On that basis, we can then all make best use of good-quality catalogue records from other libraries with the minimum of editorial change for local use. We can also ensure that our processes for creating and for deriving catalogue records are efficient, that they are effective, and that they are provided as economically as possible in accordance with the need to meet service requirements for access and control. This is a responsibility that every manager should expect to undertake, and indeed one they should undertake willingly and enthusiastically. Only when we are certain in our own mind that we are operating at optimum efficiency, and when we have a clear understanding of what we are doing and why, can we properly assess the impact of change and make an informed decision on where those changes can best be made. How well we assess our options and plan and implement change will have a direct effect on the quality of the cataloguing we achieve and receive.

To gear its cataloguing to the needs of the global bibliographic market, the library must be encouraged to think not just of what will make the record work in its own catalogue, collection and automated system, but what will make the record work in the greatest number of library systems. On the face of it, this is the sort of woolly, idealistic nonsense which has no place in a competitive, tightly resourced environment. Why should any library provide data which it doesn't use itself, or which is structured in a different way from that used in its own systems? The answer is another question: how much longer can any library continue to produce idiosyncratic catalogue records for idiosyncratic systems? If a library cannot produce 100% original cataloguing, it will have to find sources of catalogue records for the material it cannot catalogue itself. The more idiosyncratic the cataloguing policies and the systems, the less likely it will be that the library will find anywhere near a large enough supply of source records to make copy cataloguing economically feasible. This argument is long won in the public libraries and other collections requiring records for general, English-language materials. It is now being debated in the research libraries, with major collections of foreign-language, or specialist materials, which have traditionally been catalogued in-house and where in-house policies have fossilized within huge catalogues that form a critical part of the system of access for researchers. Given this past investment, it is stupendously difficult for such libraries willingly to change. Not to change, though, is to deny the future.

The time to start planning how we are to continue to enjoy good-quality cataloguing for our collections is now. Cataloguing departments are tightly resourced in terms of staff, the skills of cataloguers starting out in the profession are not advanced, and no library can catalogue 100% of its incoming material. We have therefore to look at ways in which we can obtain catalogue records from elsewhere which can be used in our catalogues; we have to look at our backlogs and the material in them so as to develop both long-term strategies for ensuring the increased availability of cataloguing for such items in the future and short-term strategies for providing some access now; we have to look at ways in which we can organize and develop our staff resources to provide in-house cataloguing for ourselves and for the global bibliographic network. We have to do all this, not just to protect our own cataloguing departments, which will otherwise wither and die, but to protect the quality of access to our individual library collections which only experienced and motivated cataloguers, working in contact with those collections and their users, can provide. The alternative is poorer quality, commercially produced records, a withering of the influence of librarians on the future organization of knowledge, and the slow death of our library standards as those institutions using bibliographic records cease to have any stake in creating them.

Sharing to survive

The most obvious way of getting more from less is to pool our resources. The desire to share cataloguing and the consequent need to standardize practice have been the driving force behind studies and revisions of cataloguing rules ever since Panizzi compiled his 91 Rules. We seem now to have reached a plateau in terms of cataloguing rule revision. There is no support for radical change or rethinking of the standards and their principles, although there are, of course, those who will continue to attempt perfection in the details. Unfortunately over-concentration on the minutiae always brings the risk of distorting the ability to see the big picture.

Attempts in the United States to initiate a national shared cataloguing programme have failed in the past. In the United Kingdom, there have been no such large-scale coordinated attempts, although we have recently seen the inauguration of the Copyright Libraries Shared Cataloguing Programme. This is an undertaking by the six libraries benefiting from UK legal deposit legislation – the British Library, the Bodleian Library, Cambridge University Library, Trinity College Dublin, the National Library of Scotland, and the National Library of Wales – to share the task of cataloguing the copyright intake. The project is interesting in that it did not involve the participants in detailed alignment of cataloguing application policies at any stage. The records, all of which go into the British National Bibliography, are created using AACR2, the name access points are selected from the BL Name Authority List, and LCSH are added to the record. Beyond those simple facts, however, the libraries have a more or less free hand in how they apply the standards.

This doubtless causes a *frisson* of excitement and concern to any library used to the tyranny of the Library of Congress Rule Interpretations. Nonetheless, the evidence shows that there have been surprisingly few problems in integrating the records supplied by the six libraries into the BNB, or the new headings into the BL NAL, and no indication that the lack of strictly defined application policies has had any detrimental effect on the ability of the records to function as high-quality means of access to any collection taking them into its catalogue.

Cooperative cataloguing

The adoption of a common cataloguing standard, AACR2, was the single most important factor in making true cooperative cataloguing a reality in the English-speaking world. The adherence by all libraries to a single standard makes the distributed production of nationally and now internationally acceptable records a possibility – even, as economic strictures draw ever more tightly round original cataloguing, a probability. Cooperation is the only way in which we will achieve an integrated library information system in which the catalogue, the acquisitions and circulation files, and the housekeeping data concerned with preservation and maintenance of the collection will reflect current, comprehensive information regarding the collection. It will be a library information system created by librarians, although not all of them will be on-site.

There are many varieties and hybrids of cooperation. What we might term the lowest common denominator style of cooperation – 'lowest' in terms of both cost, quality and time – is the 'cooperative' database in which a group of libraries put their existing catalogues together, willy-nilly. This is cooperation without the pain, but it is also cooperation with few of the mid-term and none of the long-term gains which would make it worthwhile qualitatively. Like key-word searching, it is better than nothing but not that much better. A lack of common standards and application policies leads to a failing of bibliographic integration and a serious reduction in the quality of systematic access to the cooperative database. In turn, this means that the collections represented are not being used effectively and the users are not getting the optimum return for their investment.

A cooperative programme must be based on commitment by the participants to agreed cataloguing standards, and to the acceptance of the output of any other member of the programme. The programme should impose clear obligations on those participating, in order to emphasize the importance of the commitment and to increase the determination of participants to reap the benefits of their investment. The benefits of cooperation do not come free. Cooperation must be entered into with a spirit and a vision that will disregard past parochialities in favour of the promise of the future.

Sharing is one way of increasing the pool of available records within the shortest space of time; another is to produce briefer records. The Cooperative Cataloging Council was formed in the United States in 1992 with the objective of facilitating '. . . an increase in the number of mutually acceptable bibliographic records available for use by the cooperative community'.[1] The United States, under the leadership of the Library of Congress, had defined a standard for the National Bibliographic Record as early as 1980, and this, taken together with the three levels of description that were specified in AACR2 when it appeared at around about the same time, meant that the concept of less than full cataloguing had become both acceptable and fashionable.

Library of Congress had also embarked on a programme of 'minimal-level cataloguing', to resolve the problem of materials which required bibliographic control but were not held to merit full cataloguing – or, more accurately, the cost of full cataloguing. Right from the start, economic considerations were the primary factor in the decision as to whether or not certain materials would be fully catalogued. The decision did not relate to the nature of these materials, or the requirements of their users, in any other sense than the 'value for money' which would be obtained through their cataloguing. Minimal-level cataloguing has too frequently been used for items deemed of less importance because they are not going to be heavily used. To equate degree of use with degree of value is by no means a sensible approach for any library aspiring to fulfil a research function.

The British Library adopted a somewhat similar approach in its notorious 'Currency with coverage' proposals of the early 1980s, which categorized certain copyright materials as destined to receive 'Level 1' cataloguing (that is, the description of the item would consist only of those data elements given in the AACR2 Level 1 definition). Some of these categories, quite deliberately, were of material which, even with 'full' cataloguing, would rarely have more data elements than were found in Level 1, which suggests that the 'savings' to be made were largely cosmetic.

Neither the LC minimal-level cataloguing programme, nor the British Library's Level 1 programme, was successful. They did, however, provide useful evidence and experience from which all libraries could learn. Minimal-level cataloguing was found not to allow sufficient access to materials which, by their nature, were often ephemeral or in a foreign language. Because of the programme, full cataloguing was not made available for unique and important material – precisely the sort of material which was not going to be catalogued elsewhere. The Library of Congress, the British Library, and indeed each and every library that still employs cataloguers and still acquires new materials, need to employ this scarce and valuable cataloguer resource in the original cataloguing of its unique material. However, this can happen in the current climate only if, in turn, these libraries are assured of comprehensive, high-quality sources of copy cataloguing for what can loosely be defined as general material. The growth of programmes such as the Copyright Libraries Shared Cataloguing Programme moves us in exactly that direction. The copyright material, the bulk of the bread-and-butter acquisitions for most small to medium libraries in the United Kingdom, is catalogued cooperatively. This frees cataloguing resource in all libraries, including the British Library, to catalogue more of its non-copyright acquisitions, these records in their turn feeding into other cooperative databases and bibliographic utilities for use by the wider library community.

Simplify, simplify!

'Simplification of cataloguing' is a soundbite phrase beloved of those charged with the job of getting more from less in their libraries. It needs very careful deliberation and presentation to play well with a sceptical professional audience. All too often, 'simplification' is, simplistically, interpreted by those who hear it as meaning 'less'. Simplification will mean that catalogue records will be shorter, ergo they will cost less to produce and cataloguers will create more of them. Simplification may well mean less, but the decision as to which data should be dispensed with is a difficult one. Simplification could more fruitfully be defined in terms of fewer, and more rigorously defined and presented, cataloguing rules and application policies. Such intellectual pruning, particularly of application policies, has the effect of easing the task of record creation with no loss of quality of access to and retrieval from the collection. But only if rules and policies are pruned with sensitivity and understanding of the end objectives of systematic access will the result be more vigorous and fruitful growth.

Subject cataloguing, because by its nature it cannot, like name cataloguing, be an exact science, offers a great deal of scope for simplification. There is no single 'right answer' in subject indexing, and the most practical objective for the cataloguing manager intent on ensuring optimum levels of recall and relevance from the collection is a high degree of consistency of analysis and application. Not only is consistency of subject analysis a problem at any one moment; subjects also change over time in the way they are perceived by writers and in the way they are perceived by both indexers and searchers. Current subject cataloguing standards such as LCSH are generally felt to be too firmly rooted in the card catalogue format and its requirement for linear, two-dimensional subject headings. Pre-coordinate indexing systems are a prerequisite for this form of catalogue. Automated catalogues allow a flexibility of searching which to some degree lessens the need for pre-coordinate systems, and future emphasis should be placed on the development of a controlled subject vocabulary rather than on the item-specific creation of pre-coordinated subject headings.

The danger in any discussion of ideas such as 'simplification' and 'minimum-level cataloguing' is that the exercise will be seen purely as a means to the end of saving money – that decisions will be taken on the basis of 'what we can get away with' rather than an analysis by skilled practitioners which will protect and even enhance the interests of the library users. The road to 'simplification' may have been paved with good intentions but this has not been enough to prevent a bumpy ride and a certain degree of rerouting of the journey.

Getting to the core of the matter

The 'core record' concept aims to set a standard for a bibliographic record providing the minimum data commensurate with maximum quality. It is 'core' in the sense that it gives the key data elements necessary for the catalogue record to function effectively in a standard system of access. The Program for Cooperative Cataloging, introduced in North America following ground-breaking work by the Cooperative Cataloging Council, has now defined the core record that will act as a standard for the Program. This core record differs from the minimal cataloging record provided by LC in several respects: it includes a classification number; it contains fully coded USMARC fixed field values; it has a flexible approach to the number of added entries and subject headings provided; and it includes more descriptive elements. But the core record is not 'full cataloguing'. Fewer data elements are mandatory, and fewer notes are mandatory. There are fewer added entries and no more than one or two subject headings. The PCC core record 'allows local agencies more flexibility and emphasizes judgement'.[2]

The work of defining the PCC core record has brought to light some fundamental differences between the United States and the United Kingdom and the ways in which their respective national libraries have influenced the national cataloguing tradition. 'Full cataloguing' in the United States is regarded as application, in their entirety, of both the bibliographic standards and the Library of Congress Rule Interpretations. The United Kingdom has no equivalent to the LCRI. To take just one example of the impact of the LCRI as a standard in themselves in North America, the PCC core record is said to have 'fewer' mandatory notes fields. In AACR2, all notes are optional unless specifically stated to be mandatory. The PCC core record does not have fewer mandatory notes fields than those cited in AACR, it has fewer than those mandated in the

----

LCRI. The flexibility given to local agencies and the emphasis on cataloguer judgement, both of which are newsworthy developments in the United States, have always been found in the UK library tradition.

Some of the Library of Congress Rule Interpretations, as we have seen, do not just 'fill a gap' in the coverage of the rules; they · can in fact change the rules. In moving data relating to a reproduction on microform to a secondary position and putting primary descriptive emphasis on the original, the LCRI relating to the cataloguing of microforms not only reverse the intent of Chapter 11, they interfere with a cardinal principle of the rules as they relate to all media. This category of 'rule interpretation' needs to be considered as a matter of urgency as we increase international cooperation. The LCRI have additionally tried to mitigate the differences in cataloguing increasingly apparent since the move away from case-based rules, by regulating practice on a case-by-case basis. The LCRI impose consistency even in areas where consistency is not required.

The PCC core record is the most recent attempt to define the basic set of bibliographic data without which a catalogue record cannot function effectively. Core records have proliferated at all levels of the library world. They are in essence a natural development from the ISBD and specifically from the three levels of description defined in AACR2 rule 1.0D. AACR2 makes clear that all catalogue records do not have to contain the maximum amount of descriptive data; a catalogue can work well with records at differing levels of descriptive fullness as long as none falls below the minimum level. Core record definitions have extended this concept across the whole catalogue record, covering not just the item description but the vocabulary-controlled access points and organizational data such as a classification number. Core record definitions for cooperative cataloguing programmes additionally extend the concept beyond the confines of a single catalogue, by defining a minimum level record for submission to a cooperative programme. We have already seen that this change of perception from bibliographic control inside the single library to bibliographic control without environmental frontiers has radically shifted the focus of many of our bibliographic tools and standards and the way in which they are applied. Authoritative headings are no longer based on the names, titles and subjects found within any one collection; minimal level records are no longer defined in terms of the requirements of a single library; rule interpretations relating to individual library practice start to fall by the wayside. The requirement driving all these changes is the need to share catalogue records.

Learning from the backlog

Cooperative cataloguing programmes will provide good-quality cataloguing for a wide range of material. Once a library has aligned its own catalogues and cataloguing policies with the standards to which these records are created, it is able to make use of all or any of the records in the cooperative pool. To continue to enhance the benefits of cooperative cataloguing, we need to determine which categories of material are covered less than fully by the programmes. To do so, we need look no further than our backlogs of uncatalogued material.

The previous chapter presented evidence showing that backlogs consist largely of material for which no copy cataloguing record can be found, and that this material is predominantly non-English-language material, specialist material, older material, or material with subject matter that cataloguers are not qualified or comfortable handling. As a starting point in addressing the lack of copy cataloguing in these categories, cooperative projects should be encouraged to involve those libraries creating a high volume of records for foreign-language materials. The United Kingdom is politically and economically well positioned to extend its cooperative links with its European Union partners, and should take every opportunity to do so. To set alongside the cooperative programmes for new record creation, we also need to build a more cooperative approach to retrospective conversion. This would bring into circulation a steadily growing number of machine-readable records for older materials, which would be recycled to ease yet more retrospective conversion. In this way the common pool of standard, controlled records increases and access to information is furthered.

The lack of common standards and tools outside the Anglo-American environment is a difficulty that must be addressed in a constructive and creative way. Developments such as the Consortium of European Research Libraries (CERL) project to create a database of records for European early printed books are a vital test-bed for the feasibility of multi-lingual authority files and databases of records created in the context of a variety of cataloguing standards.

The growth of cooperation means that cataloguing decisions can no longer be taken on the basis of the needs of a single library. If a library participating in a cooperative programme decides, for example, that a certain record will not have vocabulary-controlled headings, then that record cannot be used for high-quality access, without editorial intervention, in catalogues requiring authority control. Common standards have to be set for cooperative programmes, and common standards have to be applied by all participants. The process works both ways: the resulting expenditure on original record creation may be higher than it would be if the needs of the creating library alone were considered; but the savings to that library in having an available pool of records known to meet common standards and requiring no editorial intervention tips the scales by reducing the proportion of original cataloguing and catalogue maintenance that needs to be carried out.

Doing it better

With this infrastructure in place, the cataloguing manager finally needs to ensure that both the staff and the work processes in his or her library are organized to maximize the benefits of cooperative cataloguing. Within a cooperative, networked environment, local practices and a lack of uniform application policies can place limitations on effective cooperation. Goals have to be set which look beyond the purely local if we are to encourage the cooperative approach to flourish. Subject cataloguing in particular is a field in which local peculiarities have been jealously guarded, at the expense of the needs of the more general user. This is similarly the case in the descriptive cataloguing of special materials. We have to refocus the cataloguer's sense of accountability and responsibility to the user in the wider library community.

One of the major challenges facing the cataloguing manager is to motivate a group of cataloguers to unite their philosophy of providing quality access to the collections with the adoption of a range of techniques that provide increased productivity. There is a widespread and jaundiced opinion which holds that productivity can be increased only at the cost of quality. This is not generally the case, although it may possibly be so when considered in relation to original cataloguing alone. We have seen, though, that the percentage of original cataloguing is declining in every library. The cataloguing manager should not allow output rates for original cataloguing to be considered in isolation from other factors affecting the number of catalogue records produced. The cataloguing department must balance the equation that divides the items to be catalogued by the available time and resources, with the end goal of delivering the highest possible quality of service to the user community through the library catalogue.

Cataloguers should be encouraged to think about what they are doing and constantly read, learn and question their understanding of professional issues. They must be involved in change, not as passive spectators but as active participants – particularly when the change concerns matters in which they are the experts. When properly planned and executed, change reinvigorates a department. Organizations as well as individuals need a reason for being. Once that purpose is understood, a context exists in which decisions can be taken and future developments and strategies planned. A common purpose is also a motivator for collaboration and shared responsibility among staff, and is a motivating force for performance.

All cataloguing departments have backlogs. We have considered some strategies for how these might be reduced in the long term by actively encouraging cataloguing for foreign and specialist materials to be contributed to cooperative programmes. However, in the short term there are other ways of providing minimal access to backlogged material. The University of Virginia addressed the problem of its backlog by inserting 'provisional records' in the catalogue to give public access to its backlogged material of 22,000 items, 88% of which was foreign-language material. Interestingly, they found that the provisional records generated a significant increase in the number of requests for backlogged items, which were then hurried through the full cataloguing process. Access roads do indeed create traffic! The provisional records provided a level of access that allowed the material to be used, even if not to its full potential. We can share in the comforting conclusion of the study that 'a backlog that is under control and accessible is not a liability'.[3]

Full cataloguing is not necessary for users to find what they want, as long as they have some idea of what they do want, and as long as they do not want everything. When introducing minimal or provisional cataloguing to an organized system of access we need answers to two questions. First, which categories of material should receive less than full cataloguing? Second, which bibliographic data elements are mandatory for the less than full record? The answers to both questions should be as clear and as unambiguous as possible, but they should also retain an element of flexibility to allow cataloguer discretion on the treatment of any particular item. This ability to discriminate has to be introduced with care and its application managed and monitored carefully. Like the juror who avoids the responsibility of defining 'reasonable doubt' by casting aside all notions of reason, some cataloguers will never convict when the sentence is minimal cataloguing.

A good starting-point for deciding which items should receive minimal-level cataloguing is given by Sheila S. Intner: '. . . MLC should be given to stuff people will find anyway . . .'.[4] This doesn't mean things people will find in the catalogue, it means things they will find without going anywhere near the catalogue – material such as bestsellers and popular non-fiction. This kind of material is often 'minimal level' in the amount of bibliographic information it contains, and would rarely require much cataloguer-generated information even when given full cataloguing. The British Library gave Level 1 cataloguing to modern fiction and, the concept of Level 1 accepted in the national bibliography, that was probably a sensible choice. Difficulties with these minimal cataloguing records may well emerge in the longer term when new editions are published, or items suddenly receive public interest or notoriety. It may be a wise policy to upgrade minimal records as and when these situations occur.

Based on the criterion that minimal cataloguing should be given to things easily found, it follows that it should be given only to material that is browseable and publicly accessible. A user may be able to locate an item in the catalogue through a minimal-level record, but may not be able to assess the value of the item if, like a video, or computer software, it requires hardware to view its content, or if it is in closed stacks for reasons of security or age or lack of popularity.

Team cataloguing can be a partial answer to the problem of those backlogs built through cataloguer reluctance to handle certain material. By actively assigning the responsibility for the cataloguing of specific subject or language material to a team, rather than leaving it to the whim of the individual cataloguer, feelings of commitment to the group and a desire for the group to achieve its goals are fostered among its members. However teams can occasionally be disruptive of existing informal channels of communication with experts who may not be team members. More seriously, they can also lead to inconsistencies between teams in the application of standards and policies unless this is actively guarded against. Loyalty to the library and to the wider library community has to be paramount, rather than loyalty to the team.

The question of loyalties is a sensitive one for any manager of a professional, creative department where the interests of the profession usually act as a stronger motivating factor than the interests of the institution. It is the job of the cataloguing manager to set goals and targets that relate to the cataloguer's professional objectives, to be able to interpret and support those goals and targets in terms of professional objectives, and to then present the case for the achievement of professional objectives as in the best interests of the institution. As far as possible, the cataloguing manager must ensure that there is no conflict between the two. Once institutional and professional objectives are aligned, cataloguers are able to assert a positive leadership role within the context of a supportive institutional

---

framework. It has been a major failing of managers brought into a creative organization from outside that they have, by and large, wielded the axe at the easiest target instead of utilizing the skills and experience of professional staff to inform decisions on what can be reduced or changed with least impact on the fundamental objectives of the service.

Watching the work flow

If they are to pursue actively the objectives of currency and coverage for their catalogues, cataloguing managers must design workflows to take account of the growing volumes of derived or copy cataloguing, and play a lead role in building, implementing and upgrading automated systems. All too often cataloguers bend their processes and objectives to fit in with what a new system can provide, rather than insist on automated systems which do what cataloguers want them to do. Equally, what many cataloguers most desire from new systems is that they replicate as closely as possible the old way of doing things. Good technical services staff will understand the underlying nature of the bibliographic data, how it has been organized, and how it is expected to function – and above all, why it needs to work that way. They will have the vision to see new ways of approaching old problems and have the confidence to let go of the superseded.

Earlier chapters have emphasized the fact that libraries do not create the means of access to all levels of information in their collection, and never have done so. Commercial abstracting, indexing and reference tools and services have always played a part in the library and are increasingly found there in electronic form. Publicly funded bodies should certainly not subsidize the cataloguing and indexing of archives and databases produced for profit. Rather than squander resources in cataloguing what has been or should be catalogued elsewhere, cataloguing managers must campaign for the use and development of compatible standards for the cataloguing of electronic materials. Differences in principle and practice between commercial and library indexing are meaningless to the user, but they do affect the quality of retrieval. It is in the interest of the commercial sector to learn from and utilize library techniques of information organization and control in order to enhance the market value of their products to libraries, and it is in the interest of libraries to use their economic power as purchasers to prefer products and services using compatible standards and principles. This not only best serves the user of the library, it also enhances the value of standard catalogue records in the information market-place.

Gregor and Mandel, in their perceptive article,[5] ask if it is possible to both recapture the professional excitement in organizing and managing bibliographic control, and expand the professional interests and activities of cataloguers. It is certainly not only my hope but my belief that this can and must be done. Much of the professional excitement in cataloguing in the 1960s and 1970s resulted from a heady cocktail of the rapid development of automated means of bibliographic access and control, and the parallel development of a new theoretical analysis of bibliographic data, in many ways made possible by the removal of the straitjacket of the card catalogue. The professional excitement of the 1980s and 1990s lies in the development of new ways of managing bibliographic control, in the environment created by new catalogue media and new standards operating in a world of societal and economic change.

One of the subtle changes that cooperative cataloguing, the growth of a universal system of access to information, and the appearance of new formats and multiple versions are conspiring together to produce, is a shift towards the intellectual work manifested in the bibliographic item as the principal building block of the catalogue. What that future catalogue will look like, and how it might be integrated into a wider information system, is the subject of the final chapters.

References

1 Cromwell, Willy, 'The core record', *Library resources and technical services*, **38** (4), October 1994, 415.
2 Cromwell, Willy, 'The core record', *Library resources and technical services*, **38** (4), October 1994, 422.
3 Camden, Beth Picknally, and Cooper, Jean L., 'Controlling a cataloging backlog', *Library resources and technical services*, **38** (1), January 1994, 70.

4   Intner, Sheila S., 'Taking another look at minimal level cataloging', *Technicalities*, **14** (1), January 1994, 4.
5   Gregor, Dorothy and Mandel, Carol, 'Cataloging must change!', *Library journal*, **116** (6), 1 April 1991, 42–7.

CHAPTER 8
THE MESSAGE IS THE MESSAGE

Catalogues have to integrate, structure, control and maintain information about the library collection so as not to deny access to the user who, more often than not, brings imperfect and imprecise information to it. The computer allows the catalogue the fullest expression to date of its systematic structure . All previous forms of catalogue, whatever the hardware used to present them, were essentially reliant on the organization of data for linear listing and display. They allowed access by only one factor at a time, whether this was a start word from the heading for a name, a title, or a subject. The computer allows multidimensional searches not just on start words, but on embedded words from any data element in the catalogue which has been programmed to be indexed by the computer. This may be previously inaccessible data such as date of publication, or language. The organizational theories underlying cataloguing, its 'software', were developed and applied to maximize the capabilities of the hardware available at the time.

Computer catalogues are at their most efficient in searches based on known information, but less effective, because of the limitations of their screen-by-screen display, for browsing. In the same way, the electronic media are better for storing and reaching the small gobbets of hard information which answer factual searches. Users who have no such specific objective in mind will benefit from those aspects of the catalogue which enhance its ability to facilitate what we might call 'organized serendipity'. We shall discover in this chapter how, because we have not yet thrown off the legacy of the linear catalogue, we are not exploiting the potential of the computer catalogue to maximize the quality of retrieval from its inherent structure.

Electronic media, electronic access

In the past we have produced machine-readable records to provide search and retrieval access to whole items and to parts of items made available in a growing variety of media. Increasingly our catalogues are not just databases of electronic information about non-electronic information, but electronic information about electronic information as well. Databases of digitized information, text, pictures and sound, are growing exponentially. As the non-print media become increasingly widely used as a means of conveying knowledge and information, their bibliographic control becomes at the same time both more important and also more mainstream.

Film is one good example of a medium where full control of and access to differing versions is vital for the scholar and researcher. The rapid increase in the availability of film on videocassettes is adding to the problem. The differing cuts of a film are equivalent to the differing editions in which a work of literature might appear. If we are to avoid multiple undifferentiated entries in catalogues and databases, we need to have a coherent definition of edition or version or manifestation of a work, which is applicable right across the media. The medium in which a work is manifested is not the message, the message is the message. The work is the intellectual building block of the catalogue.

Film also raises particularly complex issues of authorship. Some parts of the work manifestation that is the film can be separated from it and made available separately, for example the screenplay or the soundtrack. The film is a collective work, knowingly composed for a specific purpose by a collection of individuals. In that sense the film is no different from any other collective work, but it exemplifies the difficulties which can arise when coupling access to the manifestations of a work with the requirements of a catalogue whose records are primarily structured according to conditions of authorship.

The way in which cataloguing has evolved has been moulded by the needs of individual libraries and the needs of books. These needs, and the technology available to meet them, have led to our present forms of catalogue and of catalogue record. There are now ever-increasing numbers of manifestations of works in media other than print: on tape, on disc, on CD. Luckily our cataloguing code, AACR, has as one of its basic principles a common approach to the cataloguing of all media, so we are ideally placed to adapt to this new situation with a minimum of disruption to our existing catalogues. Or are we?

Do the standards still work?

Is there any reason why the theoretical basis on which we have built our systems of organization and access to knowledge should not apply to digitized data? The medium in which digitized works are held and transmitted to the searcher differs from other media in that it presents no visible physical characteristics. The cataloguer cannot pick it up, look at it, and produce a physical description. Many people now hold that this simple fact alone undermines the whole basis of a descriptive cataloguing code built around the physical description of an item communicating the content of the work.

There are two flaws in this argument. Firstly, our systems of organization of knowledge are principally designed to give access to both bibliographic items and intellectual works. A descriptive cataloguing code such as the Anglo-American Cataloguing Rules does not philosophically centre on item description, although its structure, and the traditional linear display of the catalogue record, may mistakenly lead to that assumption. The first section of the rules produces a bibliographic description, but the second section, that dealing with the form and structure of the access points to be linked to that description and the data which underpins the intellectual structure and systematic approach to any collection of records, is based on the intellectual work carried by the item. Secondly, it is a fallacy to believe that electronic media have no physical existence. Any electronic document is stored in some form for later access and retrieval, in the same way as a voice may be stored on tape or pictures and sound on a video. The only difference is that the storage system may not necessarily be visible or hand-held. We may not feel that it is necessary to describe the digitized item; but then libraries have always contained material which they have felt does not warrant description for purposes of control or access. To prove the legitimacy of AACR as the inheritor of the Anglo-American cataloguing tradition, to provide effective access to works in whatever medium they are carried, we need to go right back to the objectives of the catalogue.

What the catalogue has to do . . .

In an important article, Martha M. Yee has investigated the concept of the work and how it has been treated in the Anglo-American cataloguing tradition.[1] Yee starts by looking at one of the principal objectives of the catalogue, which is to gather together the works of an author and the editions of a work. The works of a known author have been brought together under a single form of name of that author since at least the time of the Bodleian catalogue of 1674. This catalogue, and other printed catalogues which followed it, produced secondary groupings of the author's works on the basis of factors such as language or date of publication. In the 19th century Panizzi recognized the need to gather works of complex or uncertain authorship under a single form of title, when this varied between editions, versions and manifestations. The entries in the British Library Catalogue displayed under the heading 'Bible' are a vivid example of the value of this organizational device. Later, Seymour Lubetzky completed the picture by extending use of the single form of title – or 'uniform title' – to all works, whatever their condition of authorship, that had been published in manifestations with differing titles. Lubetzky gave the second objective of the catalogue as: ' . . . to relate and display together the editions which a library has of a given work and the works which it has of a given author'.[2]

The most recent statement of the objectives of the catalogue emerged from the International Conference on Cataloguing Principles in Paris in 1961. Clause 2.2 stated that ' . . . the catalogue should be an efficient instrument for ascertaining . . . (a) which works by a particular author and (b) which editions of a particular work are in the library'.[3] It is a principal objective of the catalogue – commonly known as the 'second objective' – that it should bring together all the works of an author, using a standardized form of that author's name, and all the editions, or manifestations, of a work, under a standardized, or 'uniform title', for that work. We shall see now how the medium of the catalogue critically affected its ability to fulfil the second objective.

... and how the medium of the catalogue stops it from doing it

Catalogues that appeared in the form of a book, whether published or not, were dependent for their order on the decisions of the catalogue editor rather than the mechanical application of filing rules. Humans are much more flexible than computers and are able to follow (and, on a case-by-case basis, adapt) extremely complex rules for the placing of individual catalogue entries. The card catalogue, whilst still allowing human error and error correction during the filing process, followed rigidly alphabetical filing rules. These placed author headings in alphabetical order, and the work titles relating to each author in an alphabetized subdivision. The growth of printed catalogue card distribution meant that, unless the purchasing library was willing to invest in substantial manual editing of the cards, their catalogues were ordered by the headings and subheadings printed on the cards. Thus, although the Library of Congress had internal rules for the organization of works within its catalogues, none of this vital structuring data was available to benefit the general public using library catalogues full of purchased LC catalogue cards. Similarly, cards produced by the British National Bibliography displayed or suppressed uniform titles on the basis of the requirements of a weekly printed bibliography, not of a catalogue. The entries in BNB were not specific to any library. Computer catalogues have made the purpose of the uniform title as a structuring and organizational device much less apparent to cataloguers and to users, but the rot had already set in during the era of the centrally produced 5 × 3 catalogue card.

The card catalogue, although it allowed for more timely and effective updating and maintenance, did not facilitate arrangement of entries under headings in a useful or certainly 'scannable' order. The sub-organization of entries in a card catalogue is entirely dependent on alphabetical filing rules, largely because no other organizational principle would be as easily visible and comprehensible to a user or filer. In tandem, cataloguing codes in the Anglo-American tradition increasingly made uniform titles optional, largely so that individual libraries could insert uniform titles where most appropriate and necessary to their own collections of works. This was a wise enough principle when all of a library's cataloguing was carried out internally, or where the proportion of bought-in records was sufficiently small to enable in-house editing of the records. It is no longer tenable in the cooperative era.

The vexed question of main entry

At this point we have to recognize that our understanding of the uniform title, and its ability to pull together all the available representations of a work, is seriously clouded by the false perceptions raised by the traditional linear display of the catalogue record and, above all, by the concept of main entry. The vagaries of main entry – the selection of one principal access point under which to place descriptive data relating to an item – can, when that single access point is for an author, lead to the separation, rather than the bringing together, of the manifestations of a single work. Martha M. Yee argues that a 'main entry', when taken as the single point in the catalogue where all the works of an author and the editions of each work are listed, consists not just of an author heading but author and title information together.[1] In catalogues which employ the concept of main entry this has of necessity to be the case, because the concept ties not just the item but the work carried in the item to a single author heading. This is a critically important point, and one which forces us to recognize the difference between the uniform title as a grouping device for works, and the manifestation title as a finding device for an item. Within the format of a linear catalogue it is acceptable to tie a manifestation title to a single author heading, but it is intellectually indefensible and now technically unnecessary to impose this straitjacket on the work. Even if we follow Yee's argument and take the author and title together as representing the main entry for a work, we still do not allow the catalogue to fulfil its objective of bringing together all the manifestations of a work – and it does not do so because of the requirements of main entry.

Linear catalogues, as we have seen, allow access only to an item description, and the grouping of those item descriptions, by one facet at a time. From the time of Panizzi onwards, the primary facet has been the name of the person considered primarily responsible for the intellectual content of the item described. When responsibility for the content is shared among more than one person, as is almost invariably the case with works carried in sound or visual media, cataloguing codes have given rules either for the selection of one of those involved as the main entry heading, or for entry under title when authorship is particularly diffuse or complex. This means that the manifestations of the works of an author or a stable group of authors are gathered together regardless of changes in title, but it also means – and this is critically important – that manifestations of works cannot be gathered together regardless of changes in authorship. We can have one or the other in the linear catalogue, but not both. The only way in which we might have both in the future is by developing a truly automated catalogue which breaks free of the restrictions of linearity and of the main entry. Depending on what we want to search for, such a system would be capable of displaying all the works of an author, whatever relationship the author may have had to that work, and all the manifestations of a work, regardless of differences in conditions of authorship between those manifestations.

In present conditions, however, this is not possible. It is generally held that in a catalogue employing the concept of main entry the way in which all the manifestations of a work are brought together is by placing descriptions of each manifestation with the uniform heading selected as the main entry. In essence, all catalogued manifestations of a work must of necessity have the same main entry heading if the catalogue is to bring together all manifestations of a work. When the rules in cataloguing codes lead to the main entry of two items under differing headings, then the rules appear to be saying that the items are manifestations of different works.

Although, as we have seen, cataloguing theorists from the middle of the century were giving as the second objective of the catalogue the relating and displaying together of the editions of a work which a library holds, AACR2, a code which, like its predecessors, was obliged at the time of its introduction to operate within a primarily linear catalogue environment, could not deliver this objective. Authorship, or responsibility for the content of a work, is the defining criterion for main entry. Thus, if a new edition of a work is presented as being by an author not responsible for previous editions, the edition is entered under the author responsible for the new edition, and a referential link is made with earlier editions. Main entry prohibits the collocation of all editions of a work – the user must rely on the vagaries of references, or the chance of continuity of title between editions, to bring the full scope of the library's holdings of the work to his or her attention.

If questions of main entry, and the need to select the heading for just one bibliographic identity from the many that may be connected with a work to function in that role, are set to one side, there is no reason why a uniform title alone should not act as the collocating mechanism for bringing together all manifestations of a work. The concept of main entry and the limiting aspects of the display of the catalogue record in linear form, with the main-entry heading at the top of the entry and the conceptually equal uniform title displayed in a secondary position – to all appearances a subdivision – has seriously impaired our appreciation of the uniform title and its function. We need to consider the vocabulary-controlled access point for the work quite separately from conditions of authorship. It is the application of the concept of main entry and the display of the bibliographic description under the main-entry heading in the examples of AACR2 – rather than anything appearing in the theoretical structure of the rules themselves – that is concealing from us the fact that a manifestation of a work by an author or set of authors who differ from those connected with another manifestation are both examples of the same work – and the catalogue must be capable of displaying together all manifestations of a work. If the concept of main entry is set aside, this is entirely feasible. The catalogue would be equally able to fulfil the objective of bringing together all the works of an author, whatever the relationship of that author to the work, and all the manifestations of a work, whatever the conditions of authorship of those manifestations.

Bibliographic relationships

The second objective of the catalogue, to bring together the works of an author and the manifestations of a work, is increasingly more important as we move away from concentration on the published unit as the building block of the collection and of the catalogue. We have to develop the catalogue so as more effectively to link manifestations of works and related works, and to distinguish the types of relationship between bibliographic data more clearly than is currently possible with the jumble of references, analytical entries, notes, multi-level descriptions and edition statements which has developed in response to changes in catalogue formats over the years. Much work has been done recently on bibliographic relationships, not least by Barbara Tillett[4] and Richard Smiraglia.[5] Once again, we learn that the technology available at the time as a medium for carrying the catalogue set the agenda for the linking devices it was possible to use. Book catalogues contained one full or 'main' entry, and references to that entry from other access points. The card catalogue introduced the possibility of an unlimited number of full (or abbreviated) copies of the entry, all headed by different access points. These were known as 'added entries', that is, they were additional to the 'main entry' at which the fullest description was to be found, placed under the heading identified as the principal heading by the cataloguing rules in force at the time. But given the possibility of two methods of providing access to catalogue data, when should an added entry be used and when was a reference more appropriate? The computer catalogue, with its much more flexible access mechanisms, fatally undermined the whole concept of main entry by making possible 'post-coordinate' rather than 'pre-coordinate' linking of data.

Barbara Tillett has defined seven types of bibliographic relationship:[6]

1. Equivalence (exact copies of the same manifestation of a work)
2. Derivative (editions, translations, dramatisations)
3. Descriptive (commentaries, critiques)
4. Whole-part (series/part, story/anthology)

5. Accompanying (supplements, indexes, parts of a kit)
6. Sequential (sequels, changed serial titles)
7. Shared characteristics (works with a common author, subject, language, etc.)

It has been characteristic of cataloguing codes in the Anglo-American tradition, circumscribed as their compilers have been by the restrictions and requirements of a linear catalogue format, that they have taken changing positions on whether these relationships apply within works or between works. Many of the relationships are extremely difficult to categorize in these terms. Equivalence relationships obviously exist only within a work, and descriptive relationships between works. But what of sequential relationships? Sequels clearly seem to be new works rather than manifestations, but a serial appearing under a new title? Derivative relationships present similar problems and have been treated in different ways by different codes and different editions of the codes. Despite the fact that AACR2 does not include a definition of a 'work', the rules themselves guide our perception of the work, the manifestation, and their relationships, in subtle and non-explicit ways.

How much can a work change, in content and medium, before it is classed as a new work? For those institutions choosing to use the code to produce catalogue records with a defined main entry – the principal bias of the rules in their current form – AACR treats translations of and excerpts and selections from a work as the same work, but abridgements and adaptations as new works. When a sound recording is made of a textual work, it is treated as the same work and its catalogue record will collocate with other records for the work; a film version, however, is treated as a new work. This is to put the case simplistically. It is also to raise the question of performance, a work within a work and an example of a nested bibliographic relationship.

Better the rudest work...

It is an interesting fact that no Anglo-American cataloguing code to date has included a statement of the objectives of the catalogue;

neither have they – up to and including AACR2 – included a definition of a 'work'. This becomes even more interesting when we consider the absolutely critical role the concept of the work plays in the theoretical groundwork of cataloguing. Using the concept of main entry as a guide, it is possible to work backwards from the rules to try to arrive at an understanding of how the composers of the code visualized a work.

By and large, a work can be found anywhere on a continuum running from a tightly organized string of words, pictures, sounds or data, to, more loosely, a structured set of ideas. A sound recording of a reading of *Hamlet*, a video of a stage production and a text of the play all represent the ideational content of the work we call 'Hamlet'. Of course, all three manifestations may well differ one from another in the way in which they present that content. Scenes may be cut by a producer, textual variants will be considered by an editor. Each manifestation expresses the creative work of others besides the original author. Writers of cataloguing rules and, indeed, each individual cataloguer applying those rules are faced with the decision as to whether the item in front of them represents a manifestation of a previously existing or a new work. The process has much in common with subject analysis, and like subject analysis is related to the degree of specificity we wish to offer our catalogue users – is the balance tipped to recall or relevance? Only when that decision has been made can the catalogue entry be structured and organized so as to fulfil the objective of relating and displaying together the works of a given author and the manifestations of a given work.

How the work is made manifest

The catalogue as a tool of bibliographic access must control both the bibliographic item and the work. The MARC record, mirroring the structure of the data on the catalogue card, favours the bibliographic description as the basic unit of the catalogue. The trend of practice in the last 30 to 40 years has been to ignore the problem of the collocation and control of works. The optionality of the uniform title, and the increase in items given title main entry, have increased the burden that the title proper – the title transcribed from the item

– has had to bear. The item title often has to function as a work uniform title, but it is not always clear when it is doing so. Uniform titles for an item may be present in one catalogue record but not in another, entirely dependent on the uniform titles policy of the cataloguing library. The end result is that confusion reigns, access to and collocation of works is not being provided consistently, and the user is losing out. Works are collocated and controlled in only a patchy and haphazard manner, entirely dependent on the condition of authorship of the particular manifestation in hand.

If we do not want a catalogue which relates manifestations of works, then we have to make do with one that locates items. This is conventionally held to be a 'finding list' rather than a catalogue, consisting of brief entries with little or no attempt to provide the vocabulary-controlled data which will bring together manifestations of works that are related in some way. Belief in the efficacy of finding lists to answer user needs speedily and cheaply is not a recent phenomenon; the critics of Panizzi's extensive editorial work on the cataloguing data to appear in the first published catalogue of the British Museum urged that a 'finding catalogue' could be produced in a much shorter time. Panizzi was able to point out that cataloguing the item in isolation from the collection meant that manifestations of a particular work and a particular edition of a work could be scattered when these manifestations were given different forms of name or title. Users wanting all the works of an author or all the editions of a work were failed by the catalogue.

Favouring the item at the expense of the work is enumerative, and it is easy. It facilitates counting, measuring and controlling physical items of stock. It is, though, increasingly inappropriate in systems and catalogues that want to give access to materials that are not hand-holdable and are not published units, and which increasingly want to focus on giving access to content rather than carrier, to message rather than medium. We need to make the switch from catalogues that give access primarily to items and secondarily to their content, to catalogues that give access primarily to works and secondarily to their manifestations.

Nonetheless, we are constantly told that the majority of user searches are 'specific-item' searches. The catalogue of a collection such as that of the British Library Document Supply Centre is based on just such a premise. The sole function of the catalogue is to get the user to the specific item he or she requests; it does not aspire to relate works or subjects or authors. Like a publisher's list or a stock control register, it is there to answer a single question. To what extent, though, are 'specific-item' searches searches for a specific item rather than searches for a specific work, the version of which (where a choice exists) is immaterial? Several studies have shown that in fact the user is interested in the work, the intellectual content carried, rather than a specific manifestation of that work. A modicum of thought will show that what appears, on the surface, to be a 'specific-item' search is actually a 'specific-work' search. The confusion arises only because most works are single manifestational. The majority of readers looking for *Pride and prejudice* will be satisfied with any manifestation of the work *Pride and prejudice*, and not be concerned with whether the work is edited by James Kinsley or R. W. Chapman. For a textual scholar, on the other hand, the variety of editions available will be critical. The market is based on the right to choose; our catalogues have to be of quality such that users who wish to exercise a choice are enabled to do so.

This suggests that the basic unit of any information system should be the work rather than the physical item. As we have seen, the physical form of the card catalogue blinkered us to the fact that this was, in fact, already the basis of our catalogues – albeit circumscribed by the limitations of the medium. Catalogues have traditionally been at the level of the 'publisher's unit', but there is no reason why they should continue to be so, and our bibliographic standards and systems do not demand that they continue to be so. Cataloguing and classification are intellectual, creative activities which can be carried out on any artefact in any medium.

The growth of copy cataloguing and the sharing of catalogue records mean that we have to establish a much more consistent approach to the collocation of manifestations of works. This is an area traditionally rife with local peculiarities and practices, which taken together have made it impractical to move towards a common set of application policies – much less agreement on a standard form of the data to be applied. The results of this failure to set a common practice on uniform titles are evident not just between libraries, but between the catalogues of a single library and even within a single catalogue. The problem grows as catalogues are increasingly compiled from a variety of record sources. Just one example is the British Library Humanities and Social Sciences catalogue. This catalogue of printed materials acquired by the British Library since 1971 has been compiled by a number of different record creation areas in the Library – the department responsible for copyright material, individual language areas of the BL, and, of course, increasing amounts of copy cataloguing taken from North American databases and elsewhere, which can use LC interpretations of AACR rules and even cataloguing rules other than AACR2. No resources have been put into agreeing a common BL policy on uniform titles or of editing records to bring them into line one with another. As a result, one of the major functions of a research library catalogue, which is to bring together manifestations of a work, has not been effectively carried out since the closure of the General Catalogue of Printed Books. The commitment of the British Library to a cooperative cataloguing future augurs well both for the future agreement of policy and for an improvement in the quality of its current catalogues.

This diversity of practice within and between libraries cannot be allowed to continue if the catalogue records we all create are to achieve optimum effectiveness in the maximum number of catalogues and databases. Catalogue records that are produced for cooperative use must follow consistent practices for uniform and collective titles, in exactly the same way as they are expected to do for name headings. We need to take the initiative and agree what that practice is to be.

A little brief authority

What percentage of items acquired by a library might be said to entail the additional effort which will go into compiling a bibliographic unit relating to a work – in other words, how many works will appear in more than a single manifestation? At a very rough guess, one might assess this at about one item in ten. The key point, though, is that there is no way of knowing in advance which works are going to appear in more than a single manifestation.

Authority control work is already a necessary process for every item, to ensure that the bibliographic identities responsible for the manifestation are accurately recorded in the catalogue, and that the manifestation is accessible through its subject content. The system is one of provision for all rather than means-testing. We have to assume that every heading we create has the potential to be used again, as the name, work, or subject recurs in another catalogued item. This principle of universality has often been criticized as unnecessary and wasteful as far as names are concerned because, unlike subjects, the majority of names never recur. Why should we go to the trouble of creating a unique, vocabulary-controlled form of name, and of producing an authority record that may never be used again? Exactly the same arguments will be made for any proposal to apply the principle of universality to uniform titles for works – but the battle here will be even fiercer, because uniform titles are not universally applied now.

The arguments in favour of authority control of all names occurring in the catalogue are basically twofold. In the first place, we cannot know in advance with even the smallest acceptable degree of accuracy which names will recur and which will therefore need to stand as collocation points to bring together all the items in the collection which have a relationship to that name. The only thing we do know is that the likelihood of recurrence is increasing as reissue in different media increases. If we were to abandon the principle of universal authority control for names in the catalogue, any resulting short-term savings would soon be squandered. If, for example, we agreed that we would produce an authority record only for names that recur, or for names that appear in a variety of forms in different publications and therefore need to have a single, controlled form established to ensure user access to all relevant works, we would immediately find ourselves right back in the middle of arguments concerning wasted cataloguer effort. Each name, as it occurred in cataloguing, would have to be checked to see if it was a recurring name, or a name which had appeared in a different form and therefore now qualified for authority control. The waste would be compounded because we would not, as with a system of universality, be recording the results of our checking and research for the benefit of future checkers and researchers, whether cataloguer or catalogue user. The authority control process invests in the future.

Secondly, a partially controlled catalogue is a non-controlled catalogue. With authority control it really is all or nothing. The user will not know which author names are guaranteed to bring together related works and which are not. There is no certainty, because there is no system. Authority control depends on total coverage for total recollection; the further you increase the coverage of the system the further you increase the levels of recall from the collection.

It is precisely this issue of partial control that has dogged our ability to consistently bring together manifestations of a work. Because the use of the uniform title is optional, it cannot and does not ensure that the catalogue collocates work manifestations, regardless of their condition of authorship. The growth of new media may well mean a growth in the rate of recurrence of a work and a much clearer case for the consistent control and application of uniform titles. In music cataloguing use of the uniform title has always been the norm rather than the exception. The growth of special collections of materials such as moving pictures or maps, and especially the extension of materials held in digital form, means that it is increasingly likely that a work access point will be required to collocate manifestations.

We have to impose universal authority control of works, but how do we do it without increasing the amount of cataloguer effort needed to create the record? We might theoretically need a uniform title to be included in every catalogue record, but what justification can there be for creating an additional field which, in nine cases out of ten, may well just duplicate the title? As an initial step we should investigate the possibility of automatically copying the title into a uniform title field, and institute procedures for checking titles as well as names against this growing authority file of work titles. We also need to develop ways of encouraging the understanding of the uniform title as equal to, and not dependent on, author headings attached to the record. One way of doing this would be to find other ways of coding main entry headings, perhaps at the indicator level rather than the tag level, thus destroying the perception that the main entry heading is superior (in all senses!) to the description and other access points.

A simple message

The users who would benefit from a catalogue based on the concept of intellectual work rather than publisher's unit, or biased towards fulfilling the second objective of the catalogue, as defined by Lubetzky, rather than the first, are legion. Users are more often than not interested in access to a work rather than to a specific manifestation of that work. Even if they do specify a particular edition, for example one taken from a citation or a reading list, they may not be aware that a more recent edition is available. A catalogue based on the principle of main entry will not necessarily bring the existence of an updated edition to the attention of a user who could benefit from it; a catalogue able to bring together all manifestations of a work, regardless of their conditions of authorship, is guaranteed to do so.

The book, or manuscript, or video, or CD, is a manifestation of the work carried by it. It may be the sole manifestation of the work, but nonetheless it is still a manifestation. The work may be manifested in other editions, or in other languages, or in other media, or in various combinations of these. It is those works, names, and subjects which appear in a multiplicity of manifestations, demanding skill on the part of the cataloguer in linking, placing and ordering them, that are most frequently sought by users. The cataloguing world can live without a definition of a work – we all have a pretty good gut feeling as to when a work is a new work and when it is a manifestation of an existing one, in just the same way that we can assess when a work needs a new set of subject authority data to access its content. That feeling is based, to a large extent, on whether or not our professional experience judges that a user would benefit from the bringing together in a catalogue search of the manifestations of a particular organized set of words, sounds or images.

Those users interested primarily in content rather than carrier will normally centre their enquiries on the entity defined as a work.

This is likely to be the case for the great majority of searches made of the library catalogue. However, although general content may be the primary sought characteristic, others will usually run it a close second. The medium of the carrier may well be the most important secondary characteristic. Someone searching for the intellectual work *Jane Eyre* may not be content with the video of a film manifestation. The catalogue needs to have an early-warning mechanism to indicate to users the medium in which the work is carried – a function normally provided by the General Material Designation, or GMD. The uniform title for the work and the GMD, working in tandem, give user access to both the medium and the message.

The intellectual organization that stable bibliographic standards impose on a collection and the systematic access to which this leads continue to be a necessary and valuable foundation for the operation of the library. The answer to the problem of improving access to the work does not lie in endless tinkering with the cataloguing rules or with the rules for their application. Technical experts now need to devise ways to encode the intellectually organized data resulting from application of the bibliographic standards so that it can be used flexibly and efficiently in the online environment, and so that it interacts with the other parts of the electronic information system. It is not the catalogue record data content that needs to change, but the way in which it is encoded, stored and manipulated.

The catalogue card was well-fitted for the information systems of its time, but for the online catalogues of today we need a much more flexible bibliographic record than an electronic version of the catalogue card. Nevertheless, the information communicated by the bibliographic record still remains the same, and it is information about the message and not the medium.

References

1   Yee, Martha M., 'What is a work?' Parts 1-3, *Cataloging and classification quarterly*, **19** (1, 2) 1994, **20** (1) 1995.

2   Lubetzky, Seymour, *Code of cataloging rules: author and title entry. An unfinished draft*, Chicago, American Library Association, 1960, ix.

3 International Conference on Cataloguing Principles, Paris, 1961, *Statement of Principles*, 1971, xiii.

4 Tillett, Barbara B., 'A taxonomy of bibliographic relationships', *Library resources and technical services*, 35 (2), April 1991, 150-8.

5 Smiraglia, Richard, *Authority control and the extent of bibliographic relationships*, PhD thesis, University of Chicago, 1992.

6 Tillett, Barbara B., 'Bibliographic relationships in library catalogues', *International cataloguing and bibliographic control*, 17 (1), January/March 1988, 3-6.

CHAPTER 9
REACHING FOR THE FUTURE

Libraries are in the business of providing the deepest and the widest possible access to their collections. As we add to and develop those collections, we also respond to the need to provide more access and gain more use. That is the ultimate target of the library, and the true measure of its success. If people get what they want from the library, they come back for more and the collection is fully exploited. If the library is easy to use, it will be used and those who use it will find out more about the collection and how to get what they want from it. The library of the future has to make the profitable avenues of access to knowledge and information easy to find and easy to follow for each serious researcher and casual user alike.

We make the collection accessible, in form and in content, through the library's bibliographic access system: the organized collection and the means of access to the collection acting together as an integrated whole. The catalogue is still the single most important cog in this system, recording the collection and providing access to its content. But as we have seen, the catalogue is both indivisible from the organized collection and, of necessity, supplemented by additional access routes to the deeper and wider content of the collection. Away from the catalogue, users who are content to browse benefit from the physical organization and classification of items on the shelves, and the careful siting of non-book materials and the hardware needed to use them.

Building an access system

A bibliographic access system has two elements: the technical infrastructure and its user interface, whether print in a book, cards in a tray, fiche in a reader or characters displayed on a computer screen; and the structured bibliographic data conveyed by the technical system. Both elements are in a state of constant development and change, and both need to work in harmony for the access system to operate at optimum levels of performance. Bibliographic data structured for a card catalogue will not necessarily work well in a computer catalogue: similarly the computer will not always make effective use of bibliographic data structured for human, rather than machine, manipulation.

Users rightly expect librarians to take care of the matter of providing access to the materials their libraries hold. It is all too easy, though, for librarians to become distracted by issues of hardware and software – the carriers of information rather than the information itself, the medium rather than the message. This is as true for the message sent by the catalogue as it is for the message sent by the collection. The variety of software available for bibliographic access systems creates difficulties on the technological front, which are very similar to differences in the structure of bibliographic data on the intellectual front. Some libraries try to present a single interface to the variety of systems they provide, and, as with the structure of bibliographic data, such consistency can be vitally important in encouraging users to have the confidence to experiment and in so doing enhance the value of the systems we provide and the collections we organize.

The Online Public Access Catalogue (OPAC) is the first version of an automated catalogue to appear. Originally limited to a kind of interactive video of the card catalogue, the latest breed of OPAC is much more like a bibliographic information system, providing access to a range of databases and tools and information services of which the library catalogue may be one item on an introductory menu. There is in all probability no common structure to these databases; the only point at which they are brought together is in a listing on the initial screen. Some OPACs, even when limited solely to providing access to the library collection of knowledge records, do this through replicating the existing variety of separate catalogues covering differing subjects, materials or chronological periods of time. Again, these separate catalogues are, by and large, not bibliographically integrated: they are not capable of seamless searching using controlled name, work, or subject terms from a single authority file. Different databases and different catalogues demand different software and different bibliographic tools to use them. We need to enhance technical and bibliographic commonalty and consistency, but we need to do this by coming together on the lowest common denominator which does not fail our users or our collections, and then working cooperatively to develop that basic standard.

I want now to look at both the bibliographic and the technical components of the bibliographic access system and how these are being developed to form the future catalogue. But before doing so, we need to consider how people use the collection, and how the way in which people search should influence both the way we organize the collection and the way we organize access to its content.

Helping the search

Librarians have to make careful choices as to how they arrange and present to their users the available physical resources. They aim to make readily apparent the range of resources available to the enquirer, and to draw attention to each knowledge record through a systematic method of organization based on the user's primary approach to the collection, which is usually by subject or by medium. Cataloguers also have to arrange and present the information in the records in their catalogues in ways which will make the intellectual contents of the knowledge records they represent apparent to users. This task is more difficult, but the means to achieve it are more flexible. The information in the catalogue record can be stored and displayed in ways which make a multiplicity of approaches available to the user. The quality of retrieval will depend, however, on the way in which the information content of the catalogue record has been created and controlled by the cataloguer.

Thomas Mann has pointed out that most searchers follow 'the principle of least effort'.[1] They set themselves very modest goals to begin with, and end their search as soon as they find a source which approximately achieves those goals. If this 'principle of least effort' does accurately represent the behaviour of most users (and personal experience tends to suggest that it does) then it is more important than ever that librarians make 'the best' information as easily accessible to users as is possible. If we do not, then the principle of least effort implies that the quality of research cannot help but suffer. There is no point in investing in materials the content of which the user cannot easily access. And access here doesn't just mean the simplistic recording of titles and authors and relying on the computer to do the rest; it means access to the most systematic, comprehensive and analytical levels that resources allow. Investment in rebuilding and extending professional cataloguing skills, in those institutions whose collections or business demands them, may produce far deeper and wider long term benefits than investment in computer hardware.

Mann has also suggested the 'methods of searching' model as the research model that most clearly emphasizes the obligation of librarians to act as facilitators and enablers. In this model, knowledge and information sources are categorized according to the way in which they are searched:

1. Controlled vocabulary searches in manual or printed sources
2. Key word searches in manual or printed sources
3. Citation searches in printed sources
4. Searches through published bibliographies (including sets of footnotes)
5. Searches through people sources (verbal, e-mail, electronic lists, letters)
6. Computer searches – controlled, keyword
7. Related-record searches
8. Systematic browsing, especially of full-text sources arranged in predictable subject groupings.

Certainly as a model for the physical organization of the library, each category allows for a distinct grouping of reference sources – of which the catalogue is the central point. Mann argues convincingly that this model best answers research questions; questions which are open-ended and have no simple factual answer and are exactly the sort of questions an organized system of access should be designed to answer. Above all, the model works for the library as it really is, now, right at this moment and for the foreseeable future. It does not idly dream of fully integrated systems of access, neither is it concerned with the nightmare of the virtual library. It is a practical model for library organization, on the basis of which we can build.

Extending the catalogue

All libraries are currently giving serious consideration to enhancing the use of both their on-site collections and remote sources of data, by the extension of electronic means of information retrieval. Of the many factors impacting on the quality and cost of electronic access the first is, of course, the provision of the hardware and software to make it possible. No doubt every library has experience of the introduction of a costly system which promised much and delivered little but bills from the service engineers. The scene is becoming more stable as standards emerge and as software defines hardware requirements rather than vice versa, but in a competitive commercial market this means we have to face the prospect of a certain degree of built-in obsolescence from software manufacturers anxious to maintain their profit levels.

There is much talk of extending the catalogue beyond the boundaries of the physical library by including in it not just the items physically available on site, but also items in electronic form to which the library gives remote access. We must be very careful indeed before jumping on this bandwagon, brightly though it is painted and hard though it may be to seem to betray the cataloguer's objective of extending quality access to all sources of information. The library should indeed give access to remote document stores and databases, but it is not within the scope of the library catalogue to include records for those remotely held documents, and it is certainly not the job of remote cataloguers to catalogue them. The bibliographic access system may well record the databases and archives to which access is available, as it may also record the other remote library catalogues to which it has access.

The OPAC is becoming more than a catalogue; it is being extended by gateways and local databases to give access to periodical indexes, special files, the catalogues of other libraries, and reference tools. This is a tremendous extension of provision which is of enormous benefit to library users. It is not, however, any more than the provision, through a single medium and in a single location, of types of information which have been available to the user in the past, in a variety of media and at a variety of locations. Library catalogues have been published and are available in print at locations where the Internet has not yet penetrated. An efficient system of interlibrary lending has long allowed the remote supply of information. Periodical indexes, archives of specialist material, and all the other files, all had an existence before they were put in digital form. The material is not new, it is just available faster and in some instances more conveniently for those to whom speed and convenience are essential.

The way in which the bibliographic access systems of the library are reaching out beyond the catalogue alone makes the need to extend the scope of bibliographic standards and to develop standard search and retrieval systems all the more important. The catalogue is, and will continue to be, the centre of the access system for any library which contains hand-holdable media. This is because any collection of hand-holdable media must be organized in some way for access; the library catalogue then completing and complementing that physical organization of materials by providing a key to their organized intellectual content.

The digital library

As libraries start to build collections of electronic texts and other digitized materials that are not hand-holdable, we need to take decisions on how we are to control and give access to these collections. The vexed question of what constitutes a version or manifestation of an electronic text, touched on in the previous chapter as a problem for all media, is doubly so in this particular form because of the ease and speed with which electronic text can be changed.

The increased use of the computer to compose and transmit works is likely to realise exactly the same advantages as were brought about by the increased use of printing – that is, standardization of content and mass distribution. Strange though it may seem, in many ways we are going back in time to the era of the manuscript – but with the added difficulty of the impermanence of the record. Hand-copied texts led to the existence of a great number of variants, but these variants were stable over time and place. Electronic manuscripts are not. Manuscripts are often multiple texts on diverse subjects, frequently with more than one work bound together. They are collections, but unlike published collections they exist by accident and not by design – they have not been brought together round a common subject or for a common purpose.

Manuscript and computer-produced documents share a surprisingly large number of characteristics. They are impermanent, and have the potential to exist in a great number of different versions. They present similar difficulties with regard to the question of their 'publication'. Their reproduction in a standard fashion is not easy to control, their provenance is often obscure, and their content is of variable quality. It may well be that many of the queries and difficulties we have in approaching the cataloguing of electronic texts might be answered by reference to Chapter 4 of AACR, the chapter handling the cataloguing of manuscripts.

And this surely leads us to recognition of the fact that in essence electronic media are exactly like all other media – they are a means to the end of carrying information, not an end in themselves. With electronically held information as with all the other information in the library, regardless of its medium, we have to decide to what level it is necessary to record and give access to the content. The answer will differ according to different collections and the differing needs of user groups, of course, but these user needs will drive the amount of resource the library must be prepared to commit and invest to provide the required level of access. The investment will be in people and in machines. Cataloguers will need to acquire specialist skills, and machines will be needed to give cataloguers access to the media and to exercise their skills.

But do we need AACR?

It may well be that there are certain knowledge records, access to which is not best served by standards such as AACR2 and the ISBDs. I would suggest, however, that this is little to do with the medium in which those knowledge records appear and much to do with the content of what they carry and the primary means of access to that content. Fundamentally, we might consider the distinction between libraries and archives. Archives are defined as repositories of documents. Documents have less extensive content than a book or video and in that sense require less organization on the part of the author or of the librarian to provide access to the content. They are, however, more complex than single works of art, single poems and single songs, all of which are effectively handled by library standards. It seems a general complaint of those librarians concerned with special materials that general standards cannot deal with the specific physical aspects of their material, whilst at the same time asserting that these standards are at fault for focusing attention on the physical item. In fact, as we have seen in earlier chapters, the standards do not focus attention on the physical item: they focus on the manifestation of the work.

A cataloguing code such as AACR2 makes no claims for use in special collections; it is a general cataloguing code which is pitched at the 'whole item' level, that is, those work manifestations which may be sought by and benefit from description of their physical characteristics. Many archived materials, such as photographs, slides, newspaper cuttings, electronic data and documents, do not fall into this category. The principle means of access to these materials has to be by subject or by a related name. Librarians have to create the access avenues of controlled vocabulary and classification of materials, and they have to make available all the access avenues listed in Mann's 'methods of searching' model. It is important to acknowledge the importance of both of these tasks – the creation of access roads and the making available of access roads – to the successful facilitation of research. Archived materials may not need standard physical descriptions, but there is no reason whatsoever why their content cannot be accessed by standard authority files of names and subjects, facilitating access through an integrated bibliographic information system.

Integrating access

Libraries in the future must plan not only for dial-in access to remote databases of digitized materials, but also for access to electronic resources held within the library itself. Graphics, for example, is a huge growth area, not just on CD-ROM but also in scanned-image databases. Providing controlled vocabulary access to collections such as these, just as with earlier slide and photograph collections, is of great importance. We have to avoid the mistakes of the past and work to integrate access to these special format collections with that available for the print collections. As with archived material, there is no reason why vocabulary-controlled data for the names and works related to non-print media cannot be added to general authority files, even though the requirements for description of the media to which they relate may differ.

Our bibliographic access systems, as they expand, will have to accommodate a growing variety of users with a growing variety of requirements. Consideration of the differing needs of data users is particularly important when providing subject access – not only in the sense of whether the need is for general or specific access, but also in the language and terminology used to deliver that access. Although the words used to express a subject may differ according to these user requirements, it is possible to provide such differing levels of access within a single logical framework of analytical principles. Such a logical framework already exists for the provision of access to names and to works and to descriptions of work manifestations.

Reducing the options

AACR needs to continue the moves inaugurated between the first and second edition to reduce alternative rules and optional rules. A bibliographic system based on the production and exchange of automated records cannot function effectively while these exist and indeed, as catalogues increasingly become more uniform between libraries and between codes and technical systems, there is a decreasing requirement for these alternative approaches. It may be that it is still necessary to include such options for the benefit of that diminishing band of libraries and collections totally independent of the cooperative sector, but in the meantime those within it have to work ceaselessly both to reduce the number of rule interpretations and to align the use of those that remain.

The benefits of cooperation and the necessity for standardization on a set of rules and application policies to make cooperation work have been a theme of this book. I have mainly concentrated on the descriptive cataloguing standard, because traditionally descriptive cataloguing has formed the quantitative bulk of the catalogue record. The Anglo-American Cataloguing Rules not only include rules for the description of work manifestations: they also set the standard for the formulation of two out of the three critical categories of vocabulary-controlled access points, names and works. The missing element is, of course, a genuine international standard for subject terms.

Setting the subject standard

Library of Congress Subject Headings have become the *de facto* international English-language subject standard because of their widespread and increasing use; nonetheless the LCSH are a set of subject terms, not a standard set of principles for creating subject terms. Earlier chapters have mentioned the repeated calls made over at least the last decade for a subject cataloguing code: made, it would appear, to no avail. It seems there are two ways to resolve this matter: either we can work backwards and develop a set of principles from LCSH, which could then act as a companion standard to AACR2, or we could radically redefine the Anglo-American Cataloguing Rules to include rules for creating vocabulary-controlled subject terms. Such a move, carried out in conjunction with other changes to the cataloguing code, would enable us to develop a two-part code: one part would be used to produce manifestation descriptions, and the second would be used to produce authority records for names, works, and subjects. The catalogue record as we know it today would cease to exist; machine links created by the cataloguer would pull together combinations of descriptions of manifestations at the time of a search.

Conveying the record

ISO 2709, an international standard specifying a record structure for the exchange of bibliographic information on magnetic tape, was adopted in 1973. The standard defines the structure of the record but not its content – which is, of course, the province of the cataloguing code – and the stimulus for its creation was the emergence of MARC. UNIMARC and the other national MARC formats are based on ISO 2709. MARC and UNIMARC also, as we have seen, focus on discrete publications. The information system of the future needs to break through this barrier of the discrete publication, on both the technical and bibliographic levels – not just because publication is an increasingly difficult function to define, but because it is too simplistic and limiting a concept for a catalogue or for an information system. We need to focus our attention on the work, ideational content which is carried by a multiplicity of physical carriers and is not tied to the concept of publication. Works are the expression of organized creativity; they demand both bibliographic analysis and technical definition to give proper access to that content.

Standard generalized markup language (SGML) is increasingly discussed as the possible technical cement for an information system linking catalogues, indexes, listings and indeed works themselves when they are created and held in electronic form. SGML is not itself a markup language, but a standard for constructing markup languages. Using the term 'document' to cover an infinite variety of organized information, SGML enables both the definition and expression of the logical structure of documents, and the naming of the components and elements which go to make up a document. Using this meta standard, it is possible to construct individual markup languages for individual kinds of document. A markup language for a specific type of document is called a Document Type Definition, or DTD.

There are three kinds of markup: procedural, descriptive, and referential. Procedural markup gives a set of processing instructions to a computer, indicating how specified components of text are to be manipulated. Word-processing software is an excellent example of such a procedural markup – and it also sounds a warning as to the problems that arise from proprietary markup standards. Descriptive markup identifies the logical components of documents, such as chapter, section, paragraph, author and publisher in the case of a book. Descriptive markup makes the marked-up document suitable for an infinity of uses and avoids the restrictive aspects of procedural markup. There are two varieties of descriptive markup, 'structural' and 'nominal'. Structural markup identifies those components that are signalled visually in some manner, such as chapters and paragraphs, nominal markup identifies named entities, both concrete and abstract. The similarity of intellectual approach between descriptive markup and descriptive cataloguing will be immediately apparent. If a catalogue record was the subject of markup, nominal markup would identify those data elements used to provide and control access. The final type of markup is referential markup which, as its name suggests, refers to information not present in the document itself.

To the extent that all three kinds of information – procedural, descriptive and referential – exist in electronic form, they exist at present in a fragmented environment which is largely based on proprietary markup and proprietary software. The catalogue which consists of MARC records is the single, important exception to this rule which, despite the variety of MARC formats, shows that libraries have by and large avoided the trap of tying themselves to a commercially dependent communications format. This means that the future is still in their hands; libraries have retained the power to take decisions on how their bibliographic information will be held and communicated. However, despite its importance to the library world, MARC is used only by this limited information community and is isolated from other information and information processing systems.

SGML would seem to offer the genuine prospect of a technically integrated information system, that is, it would be the underlying technical standard underpinning the information we use to produce catalogue records, the catalogue records themselves, and the electronic documents we will increasingly be cataloguing in the future. AACR2 has itself been encoded using one of the three SGML Document Type Definitions devised by the Association of American Publishers and issued as international standards. Such is our investment in MARC, however, and such would be the global repercussions of major changes to the way in which we hold catalogue data, that such moves would need the wholesale backing and implementation of major players in the bibliographic market. It is highly unlikely that such backing will be forthcoming in a political and economic climate where short-termism is the only game in town, where libraries have to obtain private finance for capital expenditure, and where private finance is interested in securing its profits by maintaining the status quo.

Using technology to further integration

Technology liberates us to apply the theory of organization of knowledge in ways that will radically improve the quality of information we retrieve from the catalogue and from the collection. Fred Ayres says: 'This will not be done by producing another edition of AACR. Nor will it be done by maintaining that the main entry is essential.'[2] I support these conclusions entirely, though possibly not for the same reasons! Ayres argues for a system which replaces the main entry with a 'manifestation entry'; a bringing together of all the manifestations of a work. He believes that AACR and the MARC format 'religiously follow' the concept of the main entry, because they are products of the card catalogue age which was bound, for reasons of economy, to restrict the number of access points to the record.

It is absolutely correct to argue that AACR and MARC have been unduly influenced by the requirements of main entry – as, indeed, how could they not be given that at the time of their inception they were called upon to structure and control catalogues that were almost entirely dependent on that concept for their integrity? I would draw a very clear and very important distinction between the two standards, however. The underlying philosophical structure of AACR2 is not dependent on the concept of the main entry; indeed, it explicitly allows the library to ignore the concept. It is entirely appropriate to respond that the bias of the text is towards those libraries which use the concept. The bias can be changed without undermining the fundamental principles of the code. The MARC format, however, is entirely dependent on the concept of the main entry, because it *is* entirely based on the premise that it will be used to produce a computerized catalogue record which can be output as a 5 × 3 catalogue card.

It is perfectly possible, as has been shown by Ayres and his team working on the Bradford OPAC, to assemble the data required for a catalogue based on the work and its manifestations, rather than on the main entry, from current AACR records held in the MARC format. Systems that can take existing records and manipulate them to provide more effective access and retrieval offer a much more pragmatic and practical way forward than sitting on our hands and waiting for the Second Age of bibliographic control. No single library, even the biggest and most well-endowed, has the resources or indeed the authority to develop and implement revolutionary change. We must commit ourselves to the gradualist path, but we must be clear where the path is taking us and be prepared to ruthlessly clear the undergrowth.

Creating the bibliographic access system

There is no doubt that there will be a continuation of the move from original cataloguing and in-house catalogue creation to the assembly of catalogues from records produced elsewhere, and the linking of that catalogue to other databases and the catalogues of other libraries and other collections. Given the way in which the catalogue has always acted as a locator of information, this enhanced, enlarged and extended access system will improve and energize document delivery and interlibrary lending. Moves to build systems that integrate the catalogue with the documents themselves are also to be welcomed, although obviously they are limited only to material in digitized form and are therefore unlikely ever to become the norm. However, materials which include their own catalogue, or access system, information are a much more tenable proposition.

As far as electronic texts are concerned, the text itself needs to have standard source information. This information could be used by the cataloguer in compiling the bibliographic record, or indeed it could stand as a catalogue record in its own right – each electronic document would come with its own integrated catalogue record. In many ways this would parallel and improve upon the print world, in which many books carry Cataloguing in Publication (CIP) data. Exactly as in the print world, the data would need to be treated with caution and would need to have a known provenance, but, those caveats agreed, the value of such data would be timely and economic, as is CIP. There is no reason why we should not question the assumption that bibliographic data can be delivered only in a single record structure – we need to discover ways in which we can efficiently incorporate into our catalogues the bibliographic data carried by an item we acquire.

Setting the target

The very first chapters of this book discussed the current public service obsession with targets. Targets are set not just as a goal to inspire performance but as a means of measuring achievement against a prescribed standard. Public service institutions, which have to report performance to secure funding, will automatically choose targets that it has a good chance of meeting, and indeed may go to substantial lengths to massage the figures, switch resources, or otherwise ensure that they *are* met, at least on paper. There is a great deal of cynicism about targets and league tables, which give a paper proof of improving performance often completely at odds with the public perception. Nevertheless targets will continue to be set – and rightly so, for the right targets can be institutionally and personally motivating and invigorating. It is vital that cataloguing managers have an understanding of what their real aims and objectives are, so that they can set targets for goals which need to be achieved and which will act as truly inspirational objectives for cataloguers. An astute cataloguing manager should have no difficulty in taking these same targets and presenting them to their library administrators in constructive and positive ways which will play well within and without the library.

It is also well worth the individual cataloguing department investing time in discussing, agreeing and establishing the results it wants to achieve. At its most basic, the department wants to produce records of a quality sufficient to get the user to the information he or she needs. They then need to set that requirement against available resources of time, staff and facilities. At this point, hard decisions have to be taken. It is easy to set targets based on the number of records a cataloguer can create in a given amount of time; but much less easy to measure the success or failure of real-life searches using those records in the context of the catalogue. Setting targets based on the 'more for less' principle alone may mean that the required social result of satisfied users is not achieved. Creating a catalogue that brings together descriptions of manifestations linked to vocabulary-controlled names, works and subjects by no means implies that cataloguers will spend more time in creating lengthy, abstruse records. A brief description attached to controlled access points for the work will function perfectly, whereas a lengthy, perfect description could be scattered to the wind by the failure properly to control the data giving access to the work the described item carries.

National cataloguing centres

It is logical to assume that as we push towards the concept of Universal Bibliographic Control, with each work manifestation catalogued once and the resulting record used in an infinity of individual library catalogues, there will be a diminishing need for the bibliographic record itself to be replicated. In one by no means impossible scenario for the future, it will be the job of the cataloguer to separate bibliographic information that is not copy specific, and which relates to the bibliographic work and its manifestation, from 'housekeeping' data of relevance purely to the local copy, its location and availability status. The catalogue must, of course, include information that lets the user know when and where he or she can get hold of a manifestation. This local holdings information will be linked to a remote bibliographic database, the bibliographic data in which will be centrally maintained for the benefit of all.

It is even possible to imagine the creation of an organization similar to the British National Bibliography, built around the requirement to catalogue the British published output in all media. Such an organization would receive legal deposit items centrally, catalogue them, and maintain a database of records according to agreed international standards. This database would be linked to similar national databases elsewhere. There would be long-term economies of scale, and there would be improvements in currency and quality for those institutions linking to the database. Any such future bibliographical organizations would need to be under the control, and operating with the authority of, the appropriate national library or library authority in each country. Only by maintaining that link with a publicly accountable body will we ensure the proper development of standards and the quality and consistency of application of bibliographic tools and standards. The nation's intellectual record and the ability to retrieve it are too important to be left solely to the vagaries of the market; too precious to be driven by the profit motive.

This is the plan . . .

There are three things we need to do to create a future library bibliographic access system that will provide high-quality retrieval from our collections in a timely, practical and efficient manner. Firstly, we need to work towards a common analytic approach and development path for both general and specialist bibliographic standards. Secondly, we need to extend the use of bibliographic standards and tools over a wider range of materials, and to deeper levels of information. Thirdly, we need to develop a subject approach to information which is based on principle and which can be applied in a range of products to meet a range of user requirements.

In parallel, we need to develop systems that can take this standard data and store and use it flexibly. We need to create an information system that stores unique, vocabulary-controlled identifiers for names, works and subjects, and links them to bibliographic descriptions of manifestations. We need standard access points linked to standard manifestation descriptions, and we need to encourage the greatest possible number of contributors to the bibliographic data market-place to use the same standards for creating those access points and descriptions. We need to come to some agreement as to how we might best express the data that represents a work, and how we are going to provide systematic access to works across bibliographic information systems. Above all, we should have the long-term goal of liberating our bibliographic and technical systems and standards from the need to operate on the basis of standalone bibliographic records which integrate descriptive and controlled access data in a single, fixed form.

This is not the cheapest option, and it is not the hand-built, tailored option. This is the option that gives optimum performance at the lowest practical cost. This is the option that invests in the future.

References

1 Mann, Thomas, *Library research models*, New York, Oxford University Press, 1993.
2 Ayres, F. H., 'Bibliographic control at the crossroads', *Cataloging and classification quarterly*, 20 (3), 1995, 5–18.

EPILOGUE

It is becoming progressively more difficult to engineer change. Libraries are increasingly dependent on outside suppliers for both their bibliographic and their technical system needs. Outsourcing, as it becomes ever more widespread, means that librarians are no longer able to control the future of their organized systems of access. If we cannot control our organized systems of access, we cannot control the beating heart of the library. Even the largest of libraries in the UK, if they are in receipt of public money, cannot now initiate large-scale capital expenditure without passing through processes intended to ensure private sector funding for change, wherever and whenever this is available. Private sector funding will not be available for anything other than developments that will bring profits to the private sector in the short term.

Short-term thinking has long been the malaise besetting the British financial system. Libraries, previously immune, now find they are unable to allow themselves the luxury of research, of risk taking, and of investment for the future. Those acting on behalf of our citizen shareholders demand a short-term profit, and are not prepared to commit their capital long term. We are now in the true era of the cynic; we know the cost of everything (or, more accurately, we are asked to cost everything) and the value can go hang. Even should we want to, would we now be in a position to invest resources in devising, let alone implementing, a new edition of AACR? An example of just one current development of major, long term value to the library economy, is our work to align the Anglo-American MARC formats. We have the broad support of the UK library community, but whether we can move forward and implement our decisions is in the hands of the vendors and utilities who deal in UKMARC records and systems, and what they will charge to make the change. This is the case for the British Library just as much as it is for the smallest public library. The future of cataloguing is not in the hands of librarians alone.

Within that social and economic context, we have to think and plan strategically to ensure the continuing professional quality of our library services. We need to base our strategy on a clear understanding of the purpose of the catalogue, and let this lead to a reappraisal of how we design and build a catalogue to meet that purpose. The steady reduction in original cataloguing in our libraries – particularly the public libraries – taken together with the reduction in the teaching in our library schools of the theory and practise of cataloguing and classification is a lethal combination which is undermining our professional ability positively to assert the value of what we do as cataloguers. We are losing our understanding of the skills and techniques of record creation, and of the intellectual pulling together of bibliographic information to enhance the quality of access to and retrieval from our collections. In concentrating on the means we are forgetting the end. Cooperation is, in my view, the great goal of the next decade, but we have to cooperate with a generosity of spirit and a willingness to change. We certainly need to promote economy in the use of human resources, but those savings should be at the expense of policies and processes which are not a necessary part of the systematic organization of knowledge. Only through a clear understanding of the principles of systematic organization can we make an informed and confident decision as to what we can let go.

Investing in cooperative networks has to be the major plank in our strategy to ensure a future for cataloguing. It is a long time since libraries existed in a state of independence, their systems of organization and access cocooned from the outside world. Cooperation is by no means a mere by-product of automation; automation has simply facilitated the range and extent of cooperation. Cooperation existed in the form of union catalogues and union lists long before automation brought about the online creation and exchange of records . Bibliographic utilities and institutions extra to the individual library then took the process further and developed its extent and influence. Just as networks now seamlessly link existing access systems technically, we need cooperative projects to integrate exist-

----

ing catalogue data, from a multiplicity of sources, to enhance the quality of bibliographic access for the future. By cooperating we seem to lose some influence, some perceived control over that future, but we gain the strength of numbers, and numbers give us real power. Bibliographic cooperation not only brings us the individual short-term benefit of an increased pool of records from which to draw, but also in the longer term it means the consistent development of policies and standards for the mutual benefit of us all. Constructive cooperation, in which we give as well as take, invest for the future as well as take the short-term profit, ensures our voice will continue to be heard.

Our strategy for the future must include a vision of how we want our future records to look and how we want them to work together in the future catalogue. The catalogue record attempts to express, in linear, pre-coordinated form, a combination of physical and metaphysical entities, qualities and relationships. It is not unsuccessful in achieving this objective. However, there are ways in which we can further liberate the wealth of information in the record, making the catalogue an even more fruitful source of access to the collection. The most important step is to distinguish clearly the intellectual work from the manifestation of the work.

The written word is the means by which the author speaks to us direct, with the minimum interference in transmitting the message from one human mind to another, without limit and without change. Music and drama introduce the concept of performance: the message is direct but involves the coming together, at a single location and at a single time, of performers and audience. Performance may be either live or reproduced; both are constrained by time and place. Performance on tape or disc certainly lessens these constraints but introduces the requirement for hardware and software in its reproduction.

A performance is in fact two or more contemporaneous works – the performance itself and the work, or works, being performed. A single, 'pre-coordinated' catalogue record of a performed work must have a bias to one or the other; in some media the focus is principally on the performance, in others on what is performed. A 'post-coordinated' catalogue record would not be bound in this way; the data would be coded so as to bring together all material relevant to a search at the time it was made. Given a linked system of standard descriptions of manifestations and standard access points for works, names and subjects, the cataloguer of the future will be freed from the straitjacket of creating individual records in which the relationships between data elements have to be made apparent within a linear context.

The catalogue must be capable of displaying the available manifestations of a work to the user who brings to it knowledge of a name connected with the work, a title connected with the work, or the subject matter of the work. The catalogue should initially continue to indicate locally available manifestations, but should then be able, through linked catalogue searches, to go on to list manifestations regionally, nationally and internationally. The user must be able to exercise choice between manifestations based on edition or version, content, coverage, medium, or availability.

We need to closely review AACR to establish whether the rules relating to uniform titles are properly and consistently worded to structure vocabulary-controlled access points for works. We need to change the bias of the rules as a whole towards those catalogues which are not dependent on the concept of main entry. In the same way that writers of software upgrades take their users with them step-by-step, maintaining backward compatibility as they move to new, improved ways of manipulating data, we should in the short term continue to include rules for the selection of a main entry for those catalogues and lists which still depend on the concept. Anything other than gradual change of the cataloguing rules is not a possibility in the present climate, but neither, I believe, is it a necessity. These proposals move us forward along the path, the speed at which we travel will depend on conditions en route.

We need to take a very serious look at MARC and we need to do it now. Fundamentally, we have to decide whether we are staying with the format, or whether we are going to move to an alternative such as SGML – a move that would have the benefit of facilitating the building of a consistently structured information system from the document level upwards, covering information and information about information alike. If we are staying with MARC, at the very least we have to revise it so as to ensure it handles efficiently a system of bibliographic descriptions linked to authority files of names, subjects and works. It may be that the changes involved would be of such a magnitude that it would be better to go down the SGML route immediately. Realistically, though, we have to ask what library could even contemplate such large-scale change, and what library would have the authority to implement it in a tightly controlled and increasingly interdependent bibliographic network.

If there is a moral to this tale it is that it is possible to meet the challenge of cuts, it is possible to respond to the pressures of the market without diminishing the quality of access to our collections – indeed, that quality can be improved. For that to happen we need to understand where the essence of quality lies, and we need to be prepared to see the big picture and take the risks and make the changes to get to where we want to be. I believe that this is possible only if we rediscover the basic principles of the organization of knowledge, the way in which the catalogue, the classification scheme and the collection interact to provide systematic access to intellectual works, in whatever medium that intellectual content is stored, and by whatever medium it is accessed. The seeds of our future are to be found in our past.

INDEX